4th Dimension Leadership

A Radical Strategy for Creating an Authentic Servant Leadership Culture

Ron Holifield

Published by BookLocker.com, Inc., St. Petersburg, Florida.

Printed on acid-free paper.

BookLocker.com, Inc.
2017

First Edition

DISCLAIMER

This book details the author's personal experiences with and opinions about leadership.

The author and publisher are providing this book and its contents on an "as is" basis and make no representations or warranties of any kind with respect to this book or its contents. The author and publisher disclaim all such representations and warranties, including for example warranties of merchantability and HR advice for a particular purpose. In addition, the author and publisher do not represent or warrant that the information accessible via this book is accurate, complete or current.

The statements made about products and services have not been evaluated by the U.S. government. Please consult with your own legal or HR professional regarding the suggestions and recommendations made in this book.

Except as specifically stated in this book, neither the author or publisher, nor any authors, contributors, or other representatives will be liable for damages arising out of or in connection with the use of this book. This is a comprehensive limitation of liability that applies to all damages of any kind, including (without limitation) compensatory; direct, indirect or consequential damages; loss of data, income or profit; loss of or damage to property and claims of third parties.

You understand that this book is not intended as a substitute for consultation with a licensed legal or human resources professional.

This book provides content related to leadership topics. As such, use of this book implies your acceptance of this disclaimer.

Table of Contents

CAVEAT LECTOR

What you are about to read is going to be hard. It's going to be hard for two reasons — maybe three. For one thing, it may be hard to read. You may have to read some things more than once to really understand them. I'm going to try to write in as accessible a style as I can, but there are some things that we cannot afford to dumb down. So, I may be a little verbose (*it wouldn't be the first time according to my friends and colleagues*), and some of the sentences may be long, and some of the paragraphs may seem dense. Like I said, you may have to read a few things more than once to get everything I'm saying. It's not going to be intentionally obtuse, but there it is. It might be hard.

Second, it may be hard because it's frustrating to read. I'm going to call us all out on a lot of our BS, and goodness knows there's plenty of that to go around. The way most organizations do everything from hiring to on-ramping to annual reviews…it's just terrible. And we all know it. And it's time someone said some of this stuff out loud. You may end up feeling some relief when we get around to talking about alternatives, but you'll probably have to endure some frustration about your current reality reading through some of the descriptions contained here. I know I felt that frustration writing it.

Finally, it will be hard because once you've read it you're going to have to do something about it. Right now you can claim ignorance, but after you've waded through the descriptions and suggestions I make in the body of this book…well…there's no going back after that. You can't unsee what you're about to see, and you won't be able to forget it once you've learned a better way. Reading this book is going to change you. I hope it'll make you better, stronger, braver. But you'll reach a point where:

You have to decide if you're willing to disrupt the status quo in order to create something better.

It's not going to be easy; it's going to be hard. But you can do this. I believe you can. And I believe you can make the changes I talk about.

And yet....

There will be one more thing that you'll have to do if you really want to make the most of the material in this book, and this may be the hardest thing of all. You're going to have to take this book personally.

Here's what I mean by that: You're going to read some of this and think to yourself, "Oh, I wish my boss could read this!" You're going to say, "You know who needs a copy of this book? Janice in HR. How could I anonymously slip her a copy of this? Janice must read this book!"

You must not do that. At least not at first. First you must take the material in this book personally. Act as if I'm writing this to you — not anyone else. This book is for you, not them. And here's why: you must begin by owning you're/your part of the problem.

Your boss may be a stealth incompetent. Janice may be the worst HR professional in the history of HR professionals. But you are a part of the problem, too, and you must own it. You must own that you're part of the problem, and you must own your part. As my friend John Alan Turner, a leadership coach in Atlanta, likes to say, "Until you own your part of the problem, you can't be part of the solution."

I hope and pray that this is not the kind of book that will leave you alone when you're done. The ideas in this book are going to stick with you and rattle around in your brain. You'll never go to a staff meeting or a 360 review without thinking about these ideas again.

So, let the reader beware:

Change is possible, but, if it's going to happen, it has to start with you.

INTRODUCTION TO 4TH DIMENSION LEADERSHIP

I just went to a website that sells books. You've probably heard of it. It's named after a river in South America. I typed in the word "Leadership" and got 252,222 results. There's no shortage of books on the topic.

So far, I've only scrolled down a few times, advanced a few pages, but already I've discovered hundreds of titles describing the characteristics of outstanding leaders. I've learned that great leaders are humble yet bold. They're hungry, but they always eat last. They hustle while taking their time. They know the laws of leadership, and they break all the rules.

It's dizzying really.

Many executives become enthralled with this or that compelling book on leadership and rush to implement the latest and greatest theories, replete with plenty of buzzwords, prompting front-line employees and mid-level managers to roll their eyes at yet another management flavor-of-the-month.

One senior consultant with a national firm shared what she called a "BS Bingo Card" — the BS stands for Best Seller…probably.

During "important" corporate meetings, she and her colleagues would sit, while executive leadership earnestly shared the latest company-wide strategies. Afterwards those executives retired to their mahogany offices, congratulating themselves on how intently their employees had focused and dutifully taken notes in their genuine leatherette portfolios embossed in faux gold with the latest inspirational tagline. In the meantime, the middle managers retired to their conference room to compare their "BS Bingo Cards" to see who was able to mark the most BS buzzwords used during the presentation.

Maybe Dilbert really is a documentary.

You can tell you're in a climate of "Management by BS" when you find a lot of coffee mugs, sports bottles, pens, pencils, and posters emblazoned with pithy expressions culled from the best seller of choice. These will be gleefully distributed by well-intentioned executives who sound an awful lot like John Cleese on the old Monty Python TV show: "And now for something completely different."

They're not fooling anyone. Most of the people around them know this is anything but "something completely different". This is something completely the same, only more so. Middle managers especially understand that "Management by BS" is like the weather in New England. If you don't like it now, just wait a few minutes. It'll change.

Resistance to this kind of mercurial management is problematic because after a few rounds of it, middle management becomes resistant to all change — not just the flavors of the month. So, when an organization actually becomes serious about transforming itself, their initiatives most often get derailed by those in middle management. They've heard the boy cry wolf one too many times. They're numb to the argument that, "This time we really mean it." They've been through this whole song and dance before. They were here before the latest fad, and they'll be here after it's gathering dust on the shelf.

Of course, the problem is not with best-selling books (says the guy who just wrote a book he hopes becomes a best-seller). Exceptional leaders are readers, always learning, always looking for ways to improve themselves and their organizations. Best-selling books on the topics of leadership and management can be effective tools. Instead, the problem comes when we try to implement the ideas in bestsellers by focusing on programs instead of culture. In our pursuit of a silver bullet program we can unveil with fireworks and fanfare, something that will magically transform the entire organization before the clock strikes midnight - we ignore the indispensable importance of creating an aligned value system and imprinting the cultural DNA on both current and coming generations of leaders.

Authentic and sustainable transformation isn't achieved overnight through dramatic new programs and initiatives; Authentic and sustainable transformation happens through the creation of a leadership culture that intentionally and effectively develops not just current leaders, but the next generation of leaders as well. And the generation after that. And the generation after that.

Leadership development must be long-term in scope, perspective, and strategy.

OWCH Organizations

Taking the long-view on anything requires a certain kind of intense and disciplined focus on what's happening right now. This means an organization committed to long-term leadership development pays attention to recruiting, assessing, and developing leaders who are aligned with the desired organizational culture and values. Leaders like these will nurture and protect your culture. Indeed, this is the most fundamental responsibility of any leader: maintaining a sustainable leadership pipeline of candidates who are aligned with and capable of protecting and nurturing the culture while managing constantly changing realities.

By contrast, a change-resistant organization will cling stubbornly to the Old World way of doing things. Old World, Change Hesitant (OWCH) organizations are notoriously "now" oriented when it comes to leadership development. Consequently, they unintentionally foster a culture of mediocrity, blindly sowing the seeds of future decline, even as they execute effectively on current day-to-day tactical operations. In fact, their current effectiveness is often what lulls them into thinking that because things are going well today they will continue to go well in the future.

OWCH organizations tend to offer a variety of classes on leadership and management. The content of these classes may be quite good. However, they tend to be disconnected from one another and from organizational values and culture. Furthermore, these classes are menu-driven. Employees are left to choose training classes which interest them. Occasionally, a supervisor may send them to a particular class for remedial purposes, but the roster of classes remains haphazard and poorly focused. Even with the best of intentions, classes like these will miss the mark on the leadership competencies each individual and the collective team actually need to succeed. Not only will this fail to imprint cultural values, it will actually undermine the development of a coherent organizational culture. The messaging is incoherent and fractional.

It's like being given the pieces of a puzzle without being able to see the picture you're supposed to assemble. Oh, and you're only given one or two puzzle pieces at a time.

In the absence of a culturally-inspired, values-driven, step-by-step approach to preparing future leaders, a significant number of those who are promoted lack the requisite leadership competencies which should have been developed at an earlier level. They've taken a handful of classes, but there was no sequence, no understanding of the basic building blocks of competent leadership. And in OWCH organizations, the higher an individual climbs on the corporate ladder, the more resistant he or she becomes to "being trained".

This is a recipe for institutionalized, organizational mediocrity.

OWCH organizations tend to promote someone who is good at their current job. But they fail to train them in the skills they will need to be good at their new job — which usually involves greater degrees of leadership competency. As a result, they often rise to one level of responsibility beyond their leadership ability, and there they stagnate, clogging up the leadership pipeline and costing the organization momentum.

In contrast to the well-known Peter Principle, which states that employees only stop being promoted once they have risen to the level of their incompetence, these managers may be technically capable. They're just one level beyond their leadership competency. It's not like they're terrible. Certainly not bad enough to fire. But they're not good enough to thrive as leaders either, so they end up as long-term "stealth incompetents".

Stealth incompetents are operationally functional but unintentionally nurture a culture of mediocrity due to an inability to lead.

The next generation of leaders is already in the workplace. Many of them have a different set of values, a different understanding of authority, and a different approach to work life than the current senior executives. Developing a leadership pipeline is particularly critical as today's 20-somethings begin to climb the corporate ladder. The OWCH model of "training leaders by osmosis" simply won't work anymore. It's a brave New World!

Come to think of it, it never worked that well in the Old World.

4th Dimension Leadership

4th Dimension Leadership creates a culture that recognizes the importance of leadership at every level of the organization, and intentionally develops future leaders at all levels -- from the moment they enter the organization. Every employee is a leader to be developed. Sure, their context is different. The specific leadership competencies may vary from position to position. There are differing levels of responsibility and other situationally-specific factors to consider. But everyone is a leader, and every leader can be developed further.

This is an important distinction to make: leadership competency cannot be "taught" in a traditional sense; but it can be developed. A sequential, step-by-step process can be created wherein certain, fundamental, building blocks are set in place and built upon the more a leader is developed.

4th Dimension Leadership is an organic model focused on developing leaders who will nurture and protect a values-driven culture.

A VUCA World Demands Radical Leadership

The US Army War College coined the acronym VUCA to describe the new world of Volatility, Uncertainty, Complexity, and Ambiguity. This is the world leaders must be equipped to manage. Thriving in a VUCA world demands a radical style of leadership that constantly innovates while nimbly leading and rapidly adapting. All of this must take place within a collaborative environment of trust that values and nurtures healthy relationships so the entire team can keep pace.

Describing this as *"radical"* captures the constructive tension of the word *"radical"* itself. In Latin, the word radicalis meant the roots, or foundational thoughts. In modern vernacular, the word has come to imply something extreme, something out on the leading edge. Radical leadership is appropriate, then, for those who wish to lead in a VUCA world, as it requires constant innovation and rapid change within a collaborative environment of trust that values and nurtures healthy relationships.

Leadership in our world must be both rooted and adaptable – a radical approach.

Servant Leadership – *a Radical Leadership Philosophy*

Perhaps the most radical shift in leadership philosophy over the last half century has been the rise of Robert Greenleaf's concept of servant leadership. Looking at the problems of leading in a VUCA world through the lens of servant leadership, we begin to see the tension of being both rooted and adaptable as a symbiotic relationship between two extremes. This allows the tension to become both critical and constructive.

Think about a guitar. Actually, think about the strings on a guitar. There are two extreme points to which the string is attached. As the string is held in tension between the two extremes, it becomes useful for making beautiful music. If the string gives in to one of the two extremes, it becomes useless. Music is only possible with tension.

It is the same with leadership in a VUCA world. If a leader values relationships too highly, change and innovation become restricted. No music. If, on the other hand, the leader values change and innovation too highly, relationships are damaged. Again…no music. It's allowing there to be tension between trusting relationships and innovating change — this allows for the critical and constructive tension one needs to make music.

A culture of high trust and healthy relationships is the foundation that allows an innovative leader to be daring.

A culture that values relationships while routinely adapting in order to remain on the leading edge of a constantly changing world is more likely to produce both high performance (great product) and emotional satisfaction (great process) for the team. Both extremes actually need one another in order to thrive.

The 12 characteristics of Servant Leaders beautifully balances the constructive tension of radical leadership.

LISTENING

EMPATHY

HEALING

NURTURING THE SPIRIT

BUILDING COMMUNITY

AWARENESS

FORESIGHT

CONCEPTUALIZATION

PERSUASION

CALLING

STEWARDSHIP

COMMITMENT TO THE GROWTH OF PEOPLE

Notice how the first five (*Listening, Empathy, Healing, Nurturing the Spirit, and Building Community*) are overtly focused on healthy and trusting relationships. There's our first tension point: the roots of healthy relationships.

Now notice how the next six (*Awareness, Foresight, Conceptualization, Persuasion, Calling, and Stewardship*) are overtly focused on leading change into the future. Here's our second tension point: an organization adaptable enough to stay at the leading edge.

One note: Stewardship isn't usually associated with change management. However, a commitment to stewardship must involve a commitment to a sustainable future. Decisions that look fiscally conservative to a "right now" organization are often fiscally irresponsible when viewed through a long-term lens. Seeking instant financial gratification while sacrificing the future is terrible stewardship.

Greenleaf's final characteristic of servant leaders is Commitment to the Growth of People. This is how a leader makes the culture authentic, by being devoted to growing people as leaders at every level. That kind of commitment is what enables your people to walk the talk of all 12 characteristics.

Of course, every organization wants to create a culture in which every team member is constantly growing and learning. But a desire without a plan is just a wish. If you really want to create a culture like that, you'll have to spend time creating a deliberate leadership development plan and strategically-aligned systems.

You could, of course, try to find one in any of those books we talked about at the beginning of this one. But you'll be hard-pressed to find a volume providing practical guidance on how to develop an authentic and sustainable servant leadership culture — which is why I wrote this one.

Everything you'll read here has been carefully considered and field-tested over the course of a decade. What I learned is we've been looking at the problem from the wrong perspective. So, rather than focus on a description of an exceptional leader, or a description of a well-led organization, I'm taking a far more utilitarian approach. I want to give you a reliable, nuts-and-bolts strategy for shaping your leadership culture.

4th Dimension Leadership is a practical process for growing people into authentic servant leaders.

I know that what I'm talking about is radical. In fact, I know this so well I'm just going to lean into it. This whole process can be summarized as RADICAL: Recruit, Assess, and Develop Innovative, Collaborative, and Authentic Leaders.

If you're ready to get radical, read on.

01

Servant Leadership

the underlying philosophy

In 1970, Robert Greenleaf turned the business world upside-down (or perhaps right-side-up) with his brief essay, *"The Servant as Leader"*. Since that time countless books have been written, expanding upon his simple yet profound idea that service and humility are more powerful than coercion and manipulation. Now, with the concepts of 4th Dimension Leadership, we are offering a practical strategy for developing leaders who want to authentically walk that talk. In order to do this, we must first make peace with the concept of constructive tension.

When I first got into leadership, I believed my job was to resolve tension. I believed a successful organization was one in which there would be no tension, no conflict, no anxiety whatsoever. I have come to realize that anxiety will always be present, that avoiding conflict just leads to a build-up of resentment, and that tension can actually be helpful — if it is constructive.

For example, anyone who has ever overseen a budgeting process knows that healthy organizations must have a reasonable level of cash reserves on hand for emergency purposes. However, healthy organizations also must spend money — sometimes a lot of money — to stay current and relevant. So, which is it? Do we save, or do we spend? The answer, of course, is both. But the decision we make at this time is dependent upon the healthy sense of constructive tension created by our long-term goals of both relevance and stewardship.

Either/or thinking is not helpful here. Money-related tension is not a problem to be solved. If you try to solve the tension by choosing to only spend and never save — or only save and never spend — you'll only create more problems. Managing tension requires both/and thinking, discernment, and a strong sense of timing.

As another example, we could look at the goal of establishing and maintaining healthy relationships juxtaposed with the goal of creating a culture that encourages innovation. Healthy relationships are often rooted in trust, stability, consistency — the very things that discourage innovation. Innovative cultures, on the other hand, are spontaneous, unpredictable, sometimes a little volatile — characteristics that can make healthy relationships difficult to develop.

So, which is it? Do we want healthy relationships, or do we want an innovative culture? Of course, we want both, but this is not an easy thing to accomplish. Living in that tension is not something that can be programmed or rigidly demanded; it must be articulated and modeled from the top down.

This is the kind of comprehensive and holistic approach to developing leadership competencies in senior executives (*as well as every person in an organization*) that 4th Dimension Leadership is all about. This is the strategy for creating an authentic servant leadership culture from top to bottom, and that's what sets us apart. We recognize that this stuff isn't easy. It probably won't happen overnight. It's counterintuitive and countercultural because it is willing to sacrifice short-term gains — even embracing short-term losses — for the sake of the long-term vision.

Larry Spears, former CEO of the Greenleaf Center for Servant Leadership identified 12 principles of servant leadership found in Greenleaf's essay. All of these principles will be notably present in a 4th Dimension organization.

Listening

When we think of leaders, we tend to think about great communicators or boldly decisive people who are willing and able to make the tough call when it counts. While those are vital skills for anyone in a position of authority, a Servant Leader lives out the phrase popularized by Stephen Covey, "Seek first to understand, then to be understood." Active listening is both a choice that must be made and a skill that must be continually developed.

Listen to hear not only the words but the heart.

Empathy

Such understanding, gained through actively listening to others, leads to empathy. Rather than demanding that others see things from my perspective, a Servant Leader is willing to stand in another's shoes. Certainly, I cannot ever do this perfectly; I do not have your perspective because I have not had your experiences. Still, I want to communicate my desire to relate to the way another person experiences a particular situation and the context that has shaped that person's perspectives.

I must always begin by giving the other person the benefit of the doubt, presuming that they are acting with good intentions.

Healing

In many ways this principle — which Greenleaf believed to be the most powerful of all his principles — is a natural byproduct of combining the first two. A Servant Leader understands that how we treat people always has an emotional impact that is either positive or negative, either contributing positively to a person's overall health or damaging it. Because we understand this, we will strive to make the impact of our words and actions beneficial and uplifting — even when making difficult decisions regarding personnel.

Your very presence as a Servant Leader can and should be healing.

Nurturing the Spirit

All of us have a deep human need to make a difference. Servant Leaders understand this and look for ways to help team members understand the difference they are making through honest praise and supportive recognition. Suggestions for improvement are offered in an honest and straightforward way, without harshness or personal attacks. Servant Leaders understand that most people want to be their best, although many do not understand how to achieve this and need direction, equipping, and encouragement to reach their full potential. Servant Leaders are not merely interested in helping an employee develop their professional skills. Rather, they realize that a person's spirit matters, too.

When a person's spirit is nurtured and developed, work skills naturally improve, along with the work environment.

Building Community

A Servant Leader ensures that, while goals are accomplished, they are never accomplished at the expense of relationships. On the contrary, Servant Leaders rely on the power of teams working in the context of authentic community. They recognize and honor the power of a sense of accountability, belonging, and care — the ABCs of authentic community.

Healthy relationships are what allows an organization to stay at the leading edge of innovation.

Awareness

Awareness begins with self-awareness and extends to an awareness of the potential in others. It is more than just individual awareness, however. A Servant Leader is able to look at a situation and understand the politics and power plays at work, discerning the ethics and values at stake, and determining the best course of action.

Awareness creates a compelling need for servant leaders to act upon the gap between the ideal and reality for the benefit of others.

Foresight

Tony Robbins has said, "Losers react; leaders anticipate." That may be a crass way of putting things, but one of the characteristics of a Servant Leader is the ability to understand lessons from the past, realities of the present, and the likely outcome of the current trajectory. This sense of insight and intuition gives one an ability to make good decisions in a VUCA world of volatility, uncertainty, complexity, and ambiguity. They may at times make decisions that followers do not fully understand, but trust nonetheless.

Servant leaders learn from the past, and understand the present, enabling them to anticipate the future.

Conceptualization

Servant leaders dream big dreams, and they have the ability to articulate what the dream fulfilled will look like. Looking beyond the day-to-day operations, Servant Leaders keep those big, long range dreams in mind, planning day-to-day accordingly. Moreover, they are able to inspire others to visualize a better future for themselves as well. They inspire people to dream big dreams, and, in so doing, they create a shared vision that is worth sacrificing for in order to help it become a reality.

Servant Leaders are driven by a vision for the future that is better than the current reality.

Persuasion

Servant Leaders do not primarily rely on coercion or positional authority. Instead, they understand that people are much more likely to support an idea if they have participated in the creation of it. Rather than a coerced sense of compliance, persuasion creates a far more powerful sense of commitment.

All people are to be treated with respect and dignity as fellow human beings - especially if they disagree about the issue at hand.

Calling

Servant Leaders have a natural desire to serve others and are willing to sacrifice self-interest for the sake of something bigger and more important than themselves. They long to make a difference in the lives of others. Added to this, as we've already mentioned, they can see things others often cannot see — namely, the gap between the ideal and the reality. In fact, Servant Leaders feel a burden to help close that gap. Doing so brings them a sense of joy and relief, even as it moves others into a better future. This double reward, both personal and global, draws them towards their destiny, towards the fulfillment of their deepest calling.

A sense of calling allows Servant Leaders to keep going when others might give into discouragement.

Stewardship

Because Servant Leaders are committed to serving the needs of others, they recognize that they have a responsibility to use resources, achievements, and even influence in a way that preserves the good of now while providing a better future for others. While not ignoring current realities, the very essence of stewardship is long-term in context.

It is impossible to be a good steward thinking only about the short-term.

Commitment to the Growth of People

Servant leaders do not use people; they contribute to the growth of others. A Servant Leader has the underlying hope that every person he or she interacts with will be better off for having done so. This extends beyond their tangible contributions as employees, beyond their professional development to their personal development as well. The by-product of investing in the growth of people is a learning organization which is better prepared to thrive in a constantly changing world. But you cannot be a learning organization without investing in the constant growth of people.

An organization that is not a learning organization is doomed to mediocrity.

These 12 principles undergird the concept of Servant Leadership. But it will be exceedingly difficult to create and sustain such an environment if there is no way to assess how well we are practically living out these principles. To assist in that effort, there are six key questions that provide a practical self-assessment framework to evaluate leadership culture and assure that any given decision is in alignment with our stated values. These six questions apply to all interactions with all people — including governing body members, employees, colleagues, and stakeholders:

Q 1. *Are all people with whom we interact being treated with dignity and respect as human beings?*

Q 2. Are all team members growing as servant leaders and becoming more empowered, more knowledgeable, and more effective leaders?

Q 3. Are the weakest among us being helped by our service?

Q 4. Are we strengthening the trust that senior executives and the governing body actually walk the talk of servant leadership principles?

Q 5. Are we creating a culture that is authentically embracing the highest ideals of Servant Leadership at every level?

Q 6. Are we leading in a way that is constantly transforming the organization and each team member into who we aspire to become?

These six questions are, by their very nature, holistic and intended to permeate every level and every relevant aspect of the organization. They provide the standard by which to determine whether or not any particular action is aligned with the underlying values and philosophy of Servant Leadership.

02

Redefining How We Think About

Leadership Development

"I need you to design a retreat unlike anything you have done before."

He had my attention. It was 2005, and Bill Lindley, a City Manager, had the audacity to believe his Executive Team could compete with the very best organizations in the public or private sector without limitation.

"I don't want team building," he said. "I don't want goal setting. I want to reshape HOW my team thinks. I want to redefine their frame of reference and their context for what constitutes excellence and create a framework for them to relentlessly pursue it."

He wanted an organization bold enough to use as their benchmark for excellence those who were the absolute best in their various fields. For example, he wanted to use the Texas Rangers — a Major League Baseball team worth nearly half a billion dollars — as the standard for maintaining ball fields in their Parks and Recreation department. In his words, "I know we don't have the resources that the Texas Rangers do, but they are the best there is at maintaining ball fields. I want my parks department to learn how to benchmark against them — not simply against another city doing a great job, but against the very best in the nation."

That's bold.

To help him do this we designed a retreat using Randy Mayeux as part of the facilitation team. Randy makes his living reading business books and briefing corporate leaders on leading edge business thinking. He has an amazing ability to synthesize insights and perspectives from numerous sources into a coherent understanding of larger trends and patterns. He's compelling. He's dynamic. He's one of my favorite people.

Randy set the stage with the Executive Team, helping them understand this new way of thinking about benchmarking and measuring exceptional performance. As the team wrestled through some of the practical challenges of striving for excellence instead of just trying to be above average, Randy practically leapt from his chair with excitement and began sketching something on the white board.

"Do you guys know what you're saying here?

Maslow's Hierarchy of Needs doesn't just apply to individuals...it also applies to communities and organizations.

This was the "aha" moment for me. Viewing budgets, organizational culture, and political dynamics through a community-wide lens of Maslow suddenly explained so many things about how groups make decisions. Over the next few months, this thought would not leave me alone. I began to wonder if a similar hierarchical approach to leadership development could explain why some people become exceptional leaders while others pull their organization towards mediocrity — even when they have received the same training. This pattern of thought eventually birthed 4th Dimension Leadership. It allowed me to take the "what" of Servant

Leadership philosophy and flesh out a "how" for actually creating a culture that authentically walks that talk.

A few decades ago, the "Great Man" model was the defining model of leadership. The idea was that great leaders are just born that way. You either had it or you didn't. Nowadays, leadership models have become far more populist, suggesting that anyone can become a strong leader if they learn the right set of skills.

The "Great Man" model never quite rang true, but more populist interpretations of leadership skills avoid the question of why two different individuals, both competent and intelligent, could go to the same training classes, and one would develop into an outstanding leader and the other…not so much.

Maslow showed everyone that:

Unless and until your basic needs are taken care of, you won't be able to concern yourself with higher level growth areas.

I began to wonder if this is the fundamental problem many organizations struggle with in terms of leadership development. We're trying to get leaders to master the skill set at the top of the pyramid without building a solid foundation first. Maybe top level leadership skills cannot be taught quickly because they must develop and evolve over time. There is no shortcut to the penthouse; you have to take the stairs.

Leading well at your current level of responsibility is directly dependent upon having mastered the ability to lead well at a previous level.

Maslow's hierarchy unlocked the door for a leadership development strategy that moves us from a haphazard, a la carte approach to mastering the tools for leadership to a sustainable, repeatable, systematic, step-by-step approach to developing leaders. Of course, the problem is — as is so often the case — we've never done it that way before. This kind of paradigmatic shift would require a carefully designed developmental process that is long-term in nature. It provides a consistent and meaningful continuum of leadership building blocks as an individual progressed through the organization, but it's not the kind of thing that will happen overnight. And that's what people might not like about it. We want it now.

Since this idea struck me, I have had hundreds of conversations with executives. I've asked countless questions about whether there is an essential developmental hierarchy for leadership skills that can be identified and defined with enough clarity to design an actual process through which an employee could progress. I met with public sector executives, private sector executives, nonprofit executives, human resource directors, professional trainers, organizational development managers, faith-based leaders, you name it. I spoke with people representing organizations from less than 10 employees to more than 10,000 employees.

Initially, people just shook their heads and acknowledged, "We do a terrible job of developing leaders, and we won't be able to survive very long if we don't figure out how to change that." They readily admitted, "We waste a ton of time, energy, and money on leadership training that does not produce results."

And yet none of these people ever seriously considered changing the model. This is how we do it. It's terrible and ineffective, but it's the way we do it. Old World Change Hesitant models die hard.

These conversations began to weigh on me. I began to hear the frustration. I began to see how stuck people felt. And I began to formulate a new model, which I now call 4th Dimension Leadership.

4th Dimension Leadership recognizes that all employees exercise some degree of leadership — regardless of position.

Leadership is, at its core, influence. So anyone who touches anything, anyone who speaks to anyone else, anyone who is present enough to influence what is happening is a leader at some level. They may not be a very effective leader, but they are a leader.

Furthermore, they can always improve their leadership even while remaining in their current position. For example, a customer service representative can tell a customer that their billing statement is correct and be technically proficient. But they are far more effective if they lead a customer into understanding why their billing statement is correct. A facilities maintenance worker is more effective if they lead a high level executive into understanding why it is not possible to give him a thermostat that controls only his office rather than simply telling him, "No." Leadership on the front line is very different from leadership at the top, but using relational leadership skills to accomplish their desired outcomes is still critical for maximum success.

Top performing organizations expect everyone to lead, just differently depending upon their roles and responsibilities.

4th Dimension Leadership recognizes this and moves away from the OWCH model of identifying a few potential future leaders, investing intensely in them for a short while, and ignoring everyone else. By providing structure and strategy for developing leadership competencies in all employees — applied appropriately to their current roles — 4th Dimension Leadership prepares employees and the organization itself for future growth.

What is needed is a practical strategy, a set of building blocks, a comprehensive curriculum where leadership skills are built sequentially one upon the other. This is what 4th Dimension Leadership does.

At its core, leadership is about influence.

03

4th Dimension Leadership

the fundamentals

So far you have a foundational philosophy (Servant Leadership), and a vision for what it could look like if you began developing servant leadership throughout your organization. What you do not have is a strategy, and until you have that...everything else is just a bunch more talk. Let me say it again for emphasis:

Failure to develop and implement a coherent and integrated leadership development strategy will prevent the sustainable, cultural transformation you want.

To begin with, of course, we must know the leadership competencies we want to cultivate. There are lots of ways to approach this, but I think there are four distinct leadership dimensions from which all other competencies will emerge:

Relational Leadership

Operational Leadership

Systems Leadership

Strategic Leadership

Not only do all other leadership competencies grow from these four primary areas, but I believe that these four are sequential. Human beings develop things in particular orders. For example, a baby learns to crawl first, then walk, then run. A math student learns addition, then subtraction, then multiplication, then division. The sequence is essential.

Likewise, leadership competencies are sequential. If one is relationally incompetent, strategic leadership will always elude them. Having an understanding and mastery of the basics in the four areas listed above, however, allows you to further develop skills in each area. Someone who knows the basics of Systems Leadership can always go back and hone her skills in the area of Operational Leadership. But, until she knows the basics of Operational Leadership, she will never be able move on to Systems Leadership.

This explains why OWCH managers tend to rise to their level of leadership incompetence and then stagnate there for the rest of their careers. They are continually offered training, but the training is offered a la carte — with no scope and sequence. Worse, they're often offered training that doesn't build on what they've already mastered, so they have no hope of ever being able to implement new ideas.

Leadership development in OWCH organizations is random, unfocused, and unproductive because it fails to understand the basic building blocks of both leadership and education.

In most cases, an individual's leadership competency is at a lower level than their technical competency.

Their character has not caught up to their skill set. A good maintenance worker may not be a good manager of a work team. Most aren't — at least not initially. He may not have the relational and organizational skills required to manage others. And yet, we tend to promote people based on their ability to do the job they're currently doing without thinking about whether or not they'll be able to do the job we're promoting them to do.

That was a complicated sentence, so I'll say it again.

We tend to promote people based on their ability to do the job they're currently doing without thinking about whether or not they'll be able to do the job we're promoting them to do.

Consequently, employees are promoted until they get one level above their leadership competency. The problem is that they still have the technical skills they used to do their previous job, so they may not be effective, but they're not so bad that we could justify firing them. Demoting them seems punitive, and they haven't done anything to merit punishment. But they're never going to be promoted further.

This is how the leadership pipelines get clogged up. Someone else with better leadership skills comes along, but we can't leapfrog them over someone who has been here longer and put in the time. Mediocrity becomes entrenched in the culture. Frustration sets in, because the organization that was too blind to see the missing leadership competencies in the person they just promoted is probably too blind to notice that their leadership development program is ineffective.

The only thing left for a bright person to do is go home and watch reruns of The Office, wincing every time the jokes hit a little too close for comfort.

Think how different it would be if only a manager could attain competence in the basic building blocks of leadership before being promoted.

Imagine if we thought about leadership skills more than we thought about technical and operational skills when we came to promoting someone into a position of actual leadership! The truth is, the leadership skills must be in place before the promotion; the other stuff can always be learned remedially.

A learning sequence is essential to achieving excellence in an organization's leadership development. This sequence must be coherent, strategic, and deliberate. It must involve a set of basic building blocks upon which new competencies are built, and it must be integrated so that everything an individual learns reinforces and cross-pollinates with what they've already learned.

But in order for this model to truly be transformative, it must be presented in a particular context. The context for learning must stress the values of an organization, so mastering the content is not the only end goal. The way in which a person holds the content and presents the content matters. We'll talk about the hallmarks of this context in detail in the next chapter, but for now here are what I call the Seven Unifying Principles of 4th Dimension Leadership:

1. *Treat everyone with dignity and respect in every interaction.*

2. *Select team members who strive for professional excellence in every responsibility.*

3. *Prepare for the future by developing and empowering leaders at every level.*

4. *Prepare before you promote.*

5. *Seek continuous improvement personally and operationally.*

6. *Make integrity matter most in every circumstance.*

7. *Remember that it is not just about now…it is not just about me…and it never is.*

One more thing before we get into these seven principles in depth. We've talked around this, but we should probably state this explicitly. There are some things you must possess before you can become an exceptional leader. In fact, there are some things you must possess before you can become an effective employee. We'll talk more about these later, but here are the irreducible minimums:

Personal Competency

Technological Competency

Professional Competency

If you're missing these things you'll fail at every level as both employee and leader. My guess is that if you've read this far into the book, you've got those three in spades. More later. For now, let's return to those Seven Unifying Principles.

04

Seven Unifying Principles

Before you begin to make changes to your organization, you must first acknowledge that the actual culture is determining the way your leaders lead. Not the culture you want. Not the culture you claim. The culture you currently have. Your culture is a result of the leaders you have. The leaders you have perpetuate the culture you have. The culture you have determines the way your leaders lead. It's a system.

Hear this: Contrary to everything you may have thought, heard, or said, there is no such thing as a dysfunctional system.

Your system is perfectly designed to produce the results you are getting.

What is happening in your organization is not happening in spite of what you are doing. At least to some extent, it is happening precisely because of what you're doing and how you're doing it.

Until you admit this, you will never be able to initiate substantial change.

Once you have admitted that, and you're ready to begin initiating substantial change, you must begin with your understanding of success. You've got leaders, and leaders like definitions. If you don't define success for your leaders, they'll define it for themselves. That's when things go really screwy.

Have you ever noticed how you can look at the past year's numbers and have one response while another leader looks at the very same numbers and comes away with a completely different response? Usually, that means the two of you have very different definitions of success. For example, you may be looking at employee output, and someone else is looking at employee retention. Two very different lenses.

Related to your definition of success is your corporate value system. What you value will lead you to a good, working definition of success. And, in the absence of a shared value system, each leader will utilize their own personal value system — leading them to their own personal definition of success. They may not realize they're doing this, but they'll do it.

If the person at the top of the organization does not clearly and consistently articulate and model the values they want to govern the culture, they'll never be able to develop the culture they want. Instead, each leader in the organization will create their own leadership culture within their operating unit. Their leadership culture will compete with all others, and you'll end up with an organizational mess, a disaster waiting to happen.

OWCH organizations, with their a la carte menu approach to training, create such a mess precisely because this model makes it nearly impossible to spread a coherent leadership philosophy and values. Their product is a direct result of their process.

Now, when it comes to stating your corporate values, let's be honest about something. There's not a lot of difference from one organization to another. They mostly all have the same core values. At least, they all say they do. But, like one of my mentors used to say, "Don't tell me what you believe. Let me watch you work for a while, and I'll tell you what you really believe."

The problem isn't in the core values we state; the problem is that we don't often walk the talk.

We can say we're going to value creativity and innovation, but if we only reward compliance we're not really living out our stated values. This is not to say that you shouldn't state your core values - just if you're going to go to the trouble of stating them, first make sure you're stating good ones, and, second, make sure you're willing to live them out and reward them when you catch people in your organization actually doing this stuff!

There are seven core values that are essential for transforming a culture into a truly authentic servant leadership culture. I call these "Unifying Principles" because this core value system creates a unifying framework for everything else.

FIRST

TREAT EVERYONE WITH DIGNITY AND RESPECT IN EVERY INTERACTION

It seems like common courtesy and basic human decency is waning in our society. Between talk radio and television news programs, shouting and name calling has become the accepted and assumed form of communication — especially if you disagree about something. This may be a way to get good ratings, but it's a terrible way to facilitate long-term success.

Building bridges is far more effective than building walls.

The problem is that coercion, intimidation, and bullying often work — at least short-term. Great leaders understand that efficiency and sustainability are often at odds, though. Rarely do short-term goals achieved through the brute force of positional authority endure over the long haul.

Treating people with dignity and respect keeps the long view in mind.

It may sound trite, but it's true. Incorporating the Golden Rule into a leadership values system will solve almost every "people issue" where well-intended folks are involved. Whether you're dealing with employees, superiors, peers, contractors, or customers — everyone likes being treated with dignity and respect. You simply cannot go wrong doing this — even if it's not reciprocated. In fact:

How a person responds when being verbally assaulted is the very moment when the essence of leadership character is most honestly conveyed.

My friend John Alan Turner, a leadership coach in Atlanta, says, "Leaders go first." Employees are watching. They notice how leaders respond to abusive people. Leadership character is best revealed in stressful moments. If you don't model this behavior for others, they will never believe it's a core value.

Of course, treating everyone with dignity and respect DOES NOT mean we must tolerate bad behavior or poor performance. The Golden Rule carries with it an implicit duty to confront such behavior and hold problematic personnel accountable for their actions. It may even require their dismissal from the organization — if this is the most respectful path for everyone else. You treat everyone well when you hold everyone to high standards.

Committed and well-intentioned employees whose hearts are in the right spot but who are struggling with their technical or operational competency can normally be developed into high performers through the use of assessment tools, coaching, and mentoring. They may simply be in the wrong role. Maybe they haven't been properly prepared for their current level of responsibility. This is normal and to be expected, and this can usually be handled with the tools you currently have at your disposal.

Divisive and undermining employees and (particularly) leaders who demonstrate a clear lack of commitment to your organization's core values and direction must be held accountable. If an immediate course correction is not achieved, they must be removed from the organization. You can do this while continuing to treat them with dignity and respect — perhaps by assisting them in finding an organization with which they will be more compatible — but delaying their removal fails to treat everyone else with dignity and respect and damages your credibility as a leader.

SECOND

SELECT TEAM MEMBERS WHO STRIVE FOR PROFESSIONAL EXCELLENCE IN EVERY RESPONSIBILITY

Well-equipped people who are aligned with your organizational culture and passionate about achieving excellence don't need a lot of rules. They don't need a lot of rah-rah speeches. They don't need a cheerleader, and they certainly don't need someone constantly looking over their shoulder. Too many leaders are trying to motivate their employees, when they would be better off focusing on NOT demotivating them!

Great leaders don't try to control their team; they unleash the power within the team.

You'll still have to train and equip them, but you can't take someone who isn't interested in pursuing excellence and expect anything but mediocrity from them (at best). That passionate pursuit of excellence is something a person has, or they don't. You can't teach that.

This means that if you want a culture of excellence, you must hire people who already have that attitude. Too many managers hire a resume without considering whether or not the person behind the resume fits their corporate culture. Chemistry with the culture will trump technical skills every time.

Tom Landry, the legendary coach of the Dallas Cowboys, took his team to the Super Bowl multiple times with teams built around key players — many of whom had not played football in college. He took a track star, a soccer player, a rodeo cowboy, and many other oddballs and transformed them into world champions.

How?

Coach Landry knew that he could train them in skill sets specific to a given position (running back, place kicker, full back, etc.), but he knew he could not train them to be committed to excellence. If he could find that quality, he felt confident he could supply the rest.

THIRD

PREPARE FOR THE FUTURE BY DEVELOPING AND EMPOWERING LEADERS AT EVERY LEVEL

OWCH organizations tend to be top-down command-and-control cultures (even when they think they are not). They may offer decent training opportunities for technical skills, but they virtually ignore leadership development except at the senior levels of the organization. This completely misses how a leadership culture is created. An organization devoted to leadership development at every level is going to outperform a culture in which employees are always told what to do and expected to comply at all costs.

Creating a culture that is passionate about excellence nurtures leadership at every level of the organization. But doing so demands a strategy that is in place from the moment a new employee joins the organization. Failure to do so will ensure mediocrity.

Developing leaders by osmosis is the most effective way to maintain the status quo.

There is a huge difference between a culture in which you can give your people direction and a culture in which you must give your people directions. One leads only to what you want now; the other leads to what you want most.

FOURTH
PREPARE BEFORE YOU PROMOTE

Old World, Change Hesitant organizations tend to promote people and *then* begin preparing them for the new position into which they were just promoted. This is a major contributor to institutionalized mediocrity. A lack of advance preparation for the promotion means that a newly promoted person requires a much longer ramp up period to become effective in their new position, thus wasting resources and critical time in accomplishing optimal organizational performance. Each new role has a learning curve, while the person promoted figures out the challenges, opportunities, and limitations built into her new position. Failing to prepare before you promote only makes that learning curve steeper.

More importantly, the very process of training and developing and preparing an employee for a promotion into their new position before they are actually promoted provides a valuable opportunity to evaluate the prospect's ability and readiness to take on higher level responsibilities. The net result is a dramatically higher and more reliable predictor of success in the new role, thus lowering the risk of a bad promotion.

Preparing before you promote also resolves one of the major crises of most organizations today: the desperate need for succession planning. If preparing before you promote is ingrained into the culture of your organization, succession planning is solved de facto.

FIFTH

CONTINUOUS IMPROVEMENT IN EVERY ASPECT BOTH PERSONALLY AND PROFESSIONALLY

Great leaders know that results aren't the only thing that counts. Commitment to the process and the value of continuous improvement are also critical. Results may be the way you measure success, but the core value of continuous improvement is what drives results over the long haul. An unhealthy obsession with short-term results runs counter to a culture of continuous improvement and can lead organizations to make decisions detrimental to their long term interests. In fact:

What looks like success on a one-year horizon may look like failure over a 25-year horizon.

Every decision must be evaluated within a strategic context to discern how a particular decision contributes to or detracts from the long term vision and whether or not it sets the organization up for success down the road. One hundred improvements of 1% each are usually more sustainable than a new high profile program launched amid fanfare and fireworks with the goal of increasing performance by 100%.

SIXTH
INTEGRITY MATTERS MOST IN EVERY CIRCUMSTANCE

A Chief of Police I genuinely respect told me, "You can only sell your integrity once." His point isn't just about core internal values; he was also thinking about how others — particularly employees — perceive you. Integrity is the currency which allows others to buy in to your leadership. If your currency has been devalued, it will not buy you very much.

Once you demonstrate that your integrity is flexible under certain circumstances, it creates doubts regarding your integrity in all circumstances. A leader who compromises himself, sacrifices his moral authority -- and moral authority is the most effective kind of authority you can possess if you want to lead your organization towards authentic and sustainable transformation.

The courage to face the realities of today, to hold your position with grace and respect but without compromising your core values, the rock solid and steadfast commitment to living out your core values — even when it costs you something — is precisely the kind of leadership that is lacking in nearly every sector of our world, from presidents to parents.

SEVENTH
IT ISN'T JUST ABOUT NOW...IT ISN'T JUST ABOUT ME...AND IT NEVER IS

When I first saw this phrase in a book by the great American preacher Max Lucado, I had no idea how great of an impact they would have on me. This principle has the potential to revolutionize your entire life.

The sad truth is that we live in a world where politicians have bought into the idea that the next election is the more important than the next generation, where corporations believe their only duty is to increase their bottom-line at the expense of their customers' well-being. When we only concern ourselves with right now, short term results will become the sole determinant of what is and what is not appropriate and ethical. This eventually leads to cultural decay and organizational failure.

For example, the combination of executive obsession with short term returns and selfish aggrandizement at the expense of organizational core values deeply damaged some of the largest companies in America during the Great Recession of 2008, bringing our economy to the brink of collapse.

The problem with only considering the "right now" is that we live in a world where change is one of the few remaining constants. Since that's true, we must begin to embrace the concept of Strategic Visioning. Traditional strategic planning is no longer good enough because, by its very nature, it is now-centric, presuming a linear march forward from where you are. We can no longer assume the current trajectory is automatically correct.

Strategic Visioning, on the other hand, is future-centric. It begins with the desired future state in mind, while taking into consideration a wide variety of economic, demographic and social trends that will affect the future. Obviously, if you have somewhere you want to go in the future, it helps to know where you are in the present. So, this approach will rely heavily on environmental scans, questioning everything as part of the process for defining what the organization's future should be. Then it will work backward from the desired future to the current reality, formulating a plan for how that is most likely to occur. Traditional, linear strategic planning must not be allowed to replace a clear vision or become a standard for decision making.

A strategic plan is merely a methodology for how to achieve your vision; a

strategic vision is your north star for developing a strategic plan.

They're not the same thing.

Finally, perhaps the most important thing a great leader can recognize about a Strategic Vision is that it is not about them. If the leader ever makes it about herself, the organization will fail. Great leaders — 4th Dimension Leaders — are characterized by a genuine sense of personal humility, and an unyielding commitment to advancing the mission and vision of the organization over the long term. Because of this, they know that they must not create an organization that is dependent upon one individual. Now is important. You are important. But it's not just about now, and it's not just about you.

Can we be honest about something? You know that you will not be able to hold your current position forever. Eventually, someone else will be called in to do your job. You can fight against that (and lose), or you can lean in to that and have some say in who the next leader will be. One way or another, you're going to be replaced. You can be replaced, or you can replace yourself. The choice is yours.

And while we're talking about this, I feel compelled to share another insight I'm learning even as I'm writing this. Succession planning has to be more than a program. In fact, it occurs to me that an organization committed to the overall development of all of its employees won't really need a specifically designated succession planning program.

The leadership pipeline of an organization committed to 4th Dimension Leadership becomes full by default.

05

Three Predecessor Competencies

I know. I know. I'm giving you a lot of numbers. So far we've talked about four dimensions of leadership (Relational, Operational, Systems, and Strategic). Then I gave you seven unifying principles (treat everyone with dignity and respect in every interaction, select team members who strive for professional excellence in every responsibility, prepare for the future by developing and empowering leaders at every level, prepare before you promote, seek continuous improvement personally and operationally, make integrity matter most in every circumstance, and remember it's not just about now…it's not just about me…it never is).

Now, we're going to talk about three predecessor competencies. By "predecessor competencies" I mean you must have these in your toolbox before you can work on anything else. These aren't part of our leadership development process; these are prerequisites for admission into our leadership development process.

FIRST
PERSONAL COMPETENCY

In addition to lists, you might have also figured out that I love acronyms. OWCH organizations. Living in a VUCA world. Here comes a new one: WIWAK — when I was a kid.

WIWAK, we wouldn't have to talk about a lot of the things that fall under the heading of "personal competency". Whether it is due to the coarsening of society that we talked about in the last chapter, or the introduction of "Casual Fridays", or the gradual but consistently creeping informality in every arena of life, things have changed so significantly that I know one HR director who calls her new employee training, "Don't be Stupid" training. You may not want to address these issues, but an organization which desires to thrive in the future must begin where it currently is — and that will mean talking about things like:

> Appropriate business attire
> Work hours and punctuality
> Compliance with supervision
> Respect for self, others, and authority
> Appropriate business decorum
> Professional communication styles (without profanity, slang terms, etc.)
> Ability to receive constructive criticism
> Common courtesy

That list is far from exhaustive, but I think you get the gist. Each of these areas has become an increasing challenge among new employees. They were rare in the workplace a decade ago. WIWAK, my mother would have had a heart attack if she knew I was a problem in any one of these areas!

Many of our newest workers come from very different backgrounds, some from very different cultures, some from a new generation (which can feel to some of us like a completely different culture) where there are differing ideas of what constitutes "punctuality" or "appropriate business attire". Some have little understanding of how something like their personal appearance may impact their ability to develop as a leader in the organization.

Again, you can try to fight against this, or you can understand that this is just where we are as a society. If you want to develop next generation leaders, you will have to consider including personal competency training during the on-ramping process to help them get started on the right foot. You can no longer assume they know this stuff.

SECOND
TECHNOLOGICAL COMPETENCY

Any job you ever have will come with tools you must master in order to do that job. If you're doing construction work, you'll need to master the use of a hammer or a saw or a screwdriver. You'll also need to know when to use which tool. In today's office this means computers and computer-related programs or applications. It is impossible to be effective in today's world without achieving a level of technological competency appropriate for the particular role being filled.

There are three different levels of technological competency. There's technological literacy, technological proficiency, and technological specialization.

Technological literacy is the ability to utilize the basic universal technologies essential to conducting day-to-day business operations. You may not be able to write code, but you should be able to handle a Word document. You should be able to open an email attachment. You should be able to edit something in Power Point. You should be able to read an Excel spreadsheet. These are the basics. Microsoft Office stuff. The internet. If these things are foreign to you, you will have a hard time in most workplaces.

Technological proficiency is the ability to utilize these technologies at an advanced level. Not every position needs to know everything. If your job is to answer phones and file incoming mail, you probably won't be called upon to create a mathematical formula for an Excel spreadsheet or make a short training film in QuickTime. A budget analyst needs to be highly proficient with Microsoft Excel. A senior executive only needs to be literate in it. Each position has a specific list of required competencies. We can waste a lot of time and money training people to do things their role does not require.

Technological specialization is the ability to competently utilize highly specialized technologies in accordance with the demands of the position in question. The person in charge of creating training films should know all the technology required to make a training film. No one else in the organization may know how to edit and sync background music for the training film, but if that's your job, you should know it inside and out. If you work in billing, you should know all of the ins and outs of your billing system. The woman making the training film doesn't need to know the billing system. The guy in charge of billing doesn't need to know about film editing. Stay in your lane and master the technology required to truly succeed at your particular job.

These different levels of predecessor competencies are not like leadership competencies. They're not sequential. These are position specific. It's quite possible that the higher you rise in an organization the less technologically proficient and specialized you'll need to be. Higher level executives may not need to know how the mailroom is set up. Vision casting is its own competency.

The point is that an organization committed to excellence as a core value will provide highly targeted training to ensure employees possess the level of technological competence appropriate for their position. As a general rule, this would include wide-access technological literacy training for virtually every employee, targeted medium-access training for employees needing proficiency, and very intense but limited-access training for employees who need technological specialization.

THIRD
PROFESSIONAL COMPETENCY

An accountant needs to know how to keep the books. A police detective should know how to investigate a crime. An engineer needs to know how to drive a train...or whatever it is engineers do. Professional competency means you know how to do your job.

This is going to be different for each position within an organization. The training requirements will vary widely. Many professions have specific continuing education requirements to verify knowledge, skills, and understanding are current and up to date. An organization committed to authentic and sustainable transformation will provide highly targeted and effective training for employees to ensure that they possess and maintain the level of professional competence needed to excel.

06

Four Dimensions of Leadership

FIRST DIMENSION
RELATIONAL LEADERSHIP

Relational Leadership is the foundation upon which all other leadership dimensions are built.

Funny thing about foundations: they're not usually the first thing you look at. When you're in the market for a new house, you may go online and look at the photos posted on a real estate website. They'll show you pictures of the driveway, the entrance, the bathrooms, the kitchen, the backyard. That's all the showy stuff. They don't usually post pictures of the foundation. But if the foundation isn't solid, the rest of the house may be beautiful and worthless. If the foundation is off, the whole house is a disaster waiting to happen.

So it is with relational leadership competency. You may have all the technical skills in the world and understand organizational dynamics and hiring practices better than anyone else, but, if you lack the ability to establish and maintain healthy relationships, you will eventually fall apart.

Relational leadership is often exercised "from the side" — relying on Interpersonal skills rather than positional authority.

A good leader knows that she can play the authority card very few times before she loses the relational capital necessary to get things done in a pleasant work environment. Authoritarian leaders may be able to accomplish great things, but their success is generally short-lived, and their downfall usually comes from the "friendly fire" of those who have grown weary of being treated as an inferior.

Highly effective organizations recognize this reality and train all of their employees, from front line to senior executives, in Relational Leadership skills. Doing so, creates a culture where Servant Leadership can become the norm. It's the only way to ensure what's written on the wall (your stated values) is being lived out in the hall.

Dysfunction doesn't often creep into an organization through the doors marked technical or operational incompetency. It's usually relationships that go sideways first. When that relational dysfunction comes from supervisors, managers, and senior executives, things get especially bad especially fast. In spite of this, OWCH organizations consistently fail to require Relational Leadership competency as a condition of hiring or promotion, and then they wonder why they consistently create a culture of mediocrity.

Relational Leadership includes two sub-competencies. The first is Human Relations.

OWCH organizations almost always view Human Relations training through the lens of compliance. It's something they do to cover their own behinds just in case someone wants to bring a lawsuit against them. This way, if someone wants to mistreat a co-worker, the organization can demonstrate that the individual in question did so in violation of a policy, pattern, and practice that was clearly explained to them. The only reason for these training sessions is to reduce the organization's liability in the face of possible litigation.

You can imagine how fun, thought-provoking, and stimulating these training sessions are.

Of course, you would be wise to continue offering these classes. They are critical to legal defense and often required by law. But delivering the content within a Relational Leadership context provides an opportunity to instill in your folks the core value of always treating people with dignity and respect. An organization with healthy relationships as a core value isn't concerned with mere risk avoidance and having a feasible defense against a lawsuit; an organization like that will have fewer lawsuits, fewer grievances, and a higher overall standard of performance.

People want to work where they are treated well, and people who want to work do better work with fewer distractions.

Failure to require upper management to both develop and demonstrate Relational Leadership competencies dramatically increases legal exposure should something like sexual harassment occur at mid-management or higher. More importantly, though, it's impossible to create a culture of dignity and respect if upper management doesn't know and isn't expecting the very values the organization claims to embrace and attempts to teach. Any kind of attitude which suggests that one is above taking these classes ends up communicating a lack of serious support for the stated core values. And that ends up creating a culture of compliance, going through the motions, checking the appropriate boxes, rather than commitment. Authentic and sustainable transformation can only happen when an organization is committed to the values being espoused; a culture of commitment demands that employees believe their leaders are walking the talk.

The second Relational Leadership sub-competency is Customer Service. This encompasses those skill sets which equip the employee to engage and relate with people more effectively in multiple settings. It's a comprehensive approach to creating a culture of service, and it has both internal and external applications.

Most organizations assume that Customer Service training should be limited to a small group of specific employees whose primary duty is to actually interact with "customers" over the counter or over the phone. Again, that's a variation of the compliance mindset, typical of OWCH organizations who just want to do the bare minimum in terms of training.

Customer Service isn't an add-on. Customer Service is a direct reflection of culture, and, if you're going to create a culture of outstanding customer service, you must figure out how to infuse every level of the organization with it. Allowing upper management to act as if it is above continuing to develop Customer Service skills will ensure that front line and middle management employees will comply with but never be committed to excellence in Customer Service. It will be impossible to live out your core values in a system built on compliance rather than commitment.

And then there's curriculum. Most Customer Service training curricula does the bare minimum, covering the basics and mostly teaching people things they already know. Don't settle for that. Instead, make sure your training helps employees develop a wide variety of skills so they can engage and relate with people more effectively in a variety of settings. Core content such as Conflict Resolution Skills are essential to creating an effective Customer Service culture, but those same skills are critical to Relational Leadership in general, regardless of the role of a given individual.

Training all your employees in both Human Relations and Customer Service produces better employees, employees who understand the human element of your organization, employees who work together better and work better together. On top of that, you get to find those who have the abilities they'll need in order to promote and thrive in their future roles as higher level leaders. High performing organizations will require that internal employees achieve and demonstrate Relational Leadership competency before being considered for promotion.

SECOND DIMENSION
OPERATIONAL LEADERSHIP

Operational Leadership is what many of us think about when we think about leadership in the workplace. It has to do with supervisory and managerial effectiveness, leading people, monitoring budgets, stuff like that. In this second dimension, a leader progresses from managing relationships to managing the performance of employees and then operations.

Operational Leadership must be built on the foundation of Relational Leadership. If you cannot manage healthy relationships, you cannot manage the performance of your employees and operations. Well, you could...but not very well. Get the hang of healthy relationships first, then we can talk about moving on to this next level.

And that's an important point: Relational Leadership skills will always be necessary, but managing employees and operations is a whole different level. Being an outstanding leader at this level requires a different type of development.

Again, Operational Leadership has two sub-competencies: Supervisory Skills and Managerial Skills.

Supervisory Skills are, obviously, the competencies you need to be an outstanding supervisor. At the Relational Leadership level, people extend trust primarily because of how they are treated. At the Supervisory level, trust is still connected to being treated well, but positional and intellectual authority are now added to the mix.

The transition from buddy to boss can be one of the most difficult times in the development of a leader. This is where the most dramatic change in peer relationships occurs. We train up to a thousand employees every month, and one of the most frequently asked questions we get in our introductory supervisory class is, "Why didn't anyone tell me that my buddies would hate me when I got promoted?"

Making this move from employee to supervisor requires technical skills and the ability to manage relationships well, but it also requires a particular emotional makeup to succeed. Supervisory competency tends to be the area in which mid- and upper level managers are more resistant to being trained. Perhaps they're afraid others will perceive them as weak if they attend some kind of training class and sit alongside front line supervisors. And yet, another common question asked by supervisory series participants is, "Why doesn't someone make my boss attend this class?"

OWCH organizations fail to give employees the tools they need in order to be successful once they're promoted into supervisory positions. They don't require the development of Relational Leadership competencies as a condition of promotion, and then they send mixed messages to supervisors by teaching them skill sets that they know their own boss either does not possess or does not practice.

And OWCH organizations are always confused by their own mediocrity.

As I mentioned earlier, many individuals are promoted to their level of leadership incompetency because they never develop competency in predecessor leadership dimensions. OWCH organizations tend to promote people and then prepare them for the promotion after they're already in the new role.

Contrast this with 4th Dimension Leaders who recognize that it is far better to prepare people before they are promoted. All front line employees who hope to be promoted in the future should go through a Supervisory Skills Learning Track to prepare them for promotion PRIOR to being considered for promotion into a supervisory role. It seems odd that I have to say it this explicitly. It should be common sense.

The second Operational Leadership sub-competency is Managerial Skills. This track is specifically designed for those mid-level managers who have promoted beyond first line supervisors but are not yet at an executive (department head) level. All Relational Leadership and Supervisory Skills classes should be completed before an employee participates in the Managerial Learning Track.

Relational Leadership shows itself primarily in how people are treated. In a supervisory role, this becomes leadership that depends on positional and intellectual authority. Front line employees are primarily responsible for executing tasks assigned to them as individuals; supervisors are primarily responsible for ensuring that their team executes tasks assigned to their unit. Supervisors are still concerned with the execution of tasks, but they must oversee a team and not simply manage themselves. Their responsibility is still getting things done, but their role is now to make sure it is the team that is getting the things done.

As you progress from a supervisor to a manager, positional authority increases, but the nature of the leadership exercised also transitions from positional authority into intellectual authority. Employees follow you now not just because they're told to but because they have confidence that you know more than they do. Intellectual authority comes at the managerial level because you've gained the proper knowledge and demonstrated the proper understanding, not just because you have the ability to get a team to do what their superiors tell them to do.

Managers take responsibility for operational outcomes. More than that, managers devise the best strategies and tactics for achieving those outcomes. There is a clear and logical progression of leadership sophistication and mastery through which one must progress in order to transition from employee to supervisor to manager. An employee is told what to do and how to do it. A supervisor is told what to do. A manager is told what to accomplish.

A successful organization, an organization committed to thriving and flourishing for the long term, will make sure that their managerial training equips an individual for this transition from a Supervisor who executes directives to a Manager who devises ways to accomplish designated outcomes — all while operating within the provided operating policies and systems.

A 4th Dimension organization will take all Supervisors who hope to be promoted to management roles in the future (and who have already demonstrated competency in Relational Leadership and Supervisory Skills) through a Managerial Skills Learning Track before they are ever considered for promotion. It is better to be prepared beforehand than trained remedially afterward.

THIRD DIMENSION
SYSTEMS LEADERSHIP

Systems Leadership understands that everything in your organization is part of a system. Like a spider's web, it is impossible to tug on one part without affecting all the other parts. Systems govern how all the underlying operations are managed, so it is vitally important to design and implement a strategy for ensuring the effective functioning of healthy systems.

This, again, requires a significant shift in thinking and focus for a leader. In this Third Dimension, a leader transitions from managing daily operations to creating an operational environment that forms a culture which lives out the core values of your organization. Even the most routine and seemingly banal things are, at their heart, determinants of culture and core values.

The system you have created is perfectly designed to produce the results you are getting.

In other words, the culture you have is not in place in spite of what you are doing but, at least to some extent, precisely because of what you are doing and how you are doing it.

That may not be the most pleasant thought for you to consider, but it is true nonetheless. Everything that is happening — from the amount of grievances filed by employees against their co-workers to the rate of turnover you have among your staff to the overall morale of your workforce — it is all a direct result of the system you have created. And, if you want to change any of those things I just mentioned, you must change the system causing them.

Furthermore, your outcomes really reveal the health of your systems. If you have unhealthy outcomes, it is because your system is unhealthy. There is no other explanation. This is why it is so critically important to ensure that the stated core values are being lived out at every level of the organization.

Make sure that what is written on the wall is being lived out in the hall.

Systems Leadership builds upon the foundation of excellence provided in the realms of, first, Relational Leadership and, then, Operational Leadership. The natural progression now goes from Intellectual Authority to Moral Authority. Your followers not only trust that you know the right thing but that you'll also do the right thing. Success in the realm of Systems Leadership requires an individual who will embody the ethics of the organization. Only an individual committed to this can create systems through which the organization's core values will be put into practice.

Trust is required if employees are to have confidence in the integrity of the systems.

Even if they do not agree with any given decision, if employees respect the decision maker they are more likely to continue following because they believe the leader knows more than they do and is making decisions in the best interest of everyone involved.

Authentic transformation requires healthy, well-designed systems which are capable of sustaining the culture and core values, regardless of personnel changes. Organizations will only experience long-term success if they are able to grow beyond their dependence upon individual personalities. 4th Dimension Leadership is designed to create self-sustaining systems that do not depend on the specific actions of any single leader.

Your organizational systems are what enable you to translate core values into actual practice.

The leadership skills necessary to do so will build upon the competencies gained through mastery of Operational Leadership. An employee is told what to do and how to do it. A Supervisor is told what to do. A Manager is told what to accomplish. A Systems Leader (typically a department head or above) is responsible for designing, implementing, and overseeing systems which ensure organizational goals are being achieved. This work is frequently done across various organizational lines and silos.

In other words, at the Operational Leadership level, the primary emphasis is on meeting tactical objectives, while at the

Systems Leadership level, the emphasis shifts to creating systems which ensure that operational objectives are being met while maintaining a broader focus on the achievement of "big picture" goals which encompass more than just daily operations, all while staying within the philosophical and behavioral context of the organization's cultural norms and stated core values.

As with the other dimensions, Systems Leadership has two sub-competencies: Values Alignment and Systems Building.

Values Alignment is measured by the degree to which the organization truly believes and trusts that leaders are authentically walking the talk of their stated core values. That kind of trust is never static; every single action either strengthens or weakens the trust relationship.

To create values aligned systems, leaders must nurture a culture marked by healthy relationships and a trust-based leadership style.

A Values Alignment Learning Track must be completed prior to a Systems Development Learning Track in order to ensure that a high level of trust is in place. Trust is what allows organizations to function in healthy ways, innovating when necessary and navigating the speed of change. Trust is also a prerequisite for building and maintaining effective organizational systems that reinforce and support the stated core values.

All Managers who hope to be promoted to executive roles in the future (and who have already completed Relational and Operational Leadership tracks) will go through a Values Alignment Learning Track before they will be considered for promotion. There is a clear sequence in place.

Systems Building focuses on the practical, "how to" aspects of building systems that are reliable, trustworthy, and effective. It will not be enough to know that systems are at work in your organization; in order to be a great executive leader, you must also understand how systems function and how you, as an individual, affect the systems in place. It is absolutely critical that all predecessor leadership competencies have been achieved prior to taking the Systems Building Learning Track.

All Managers who hope to be promoted to executive roles in the future (and who have already completed their Relational and Operational Leadership training, as well as the Values Alignment Learning Track) will go through the Systems Building Learning Track before they will be considered for promotion. Again, 4th Dimension Leadership requires a strict sequence here.

FOURTH DIMENSION
STRATEGIC LEADERSHIP

Strategic Leadership is how an organization goes from what it is to what it wants to be.

Wanting to be better is good, but a dream without a plan is little more than wishful thinking. All the aspirations in the world will come to nothing without a good, solid strategy. But a good, solid strategy needs an end goal. Where are we headed? What do we want to do? Who do we want to be? These questions must be answered before we can decide how we're going to get there.

Vision first, then strategy. Strategic Leaders keep both in mind.

Simon Sinek has discussed this eloquently. He says that most organizations know what they're doing and how they're going to do it, but precious few understand why they're doing what they're doing the way they're doing it. It's probably not overstating things to say that few know why they're doing anything at all, but this is the critical factor that separates the great from the good, the exceptional from the forgettable, the world-changers from the also-rans.

Inspired leaders and inspired organizations will always be able to explain their purpose.

This bedrock sense of purpose will drive them to create innovative tactics (how) to accomplish their goals (what). With that clarity of vision, they can relentlessly pursue the end they have in mind while holding loosely to their methods, adapting as needed.

This kind of leadership requires a long-term, change-friendly perspective. Strategic Leaders help an organization envision a better future and develop a practical, achievable, aggressive, step-by-step plan for turning its dreams into reality.

Strategic Leaders understand the difference between a vision and a plan.

The ability to map out a plan of action (Strategic Planning or Business Execution Planning) is critical at earlier levels of leadership (particularly at the Operational Level) as you detail how you are going to accomplish the task at hand. At the Strategic Leadership level, however, the focus shifts from planning to visioning. Lower levels are focused on HOW; this level is focused on WHAT because they have a crystal clear WHY. Why does our organization exist? Who does the organization want to become? Answer those first, and then enlist the help of others in figuring out how you're going to get there.

A 4th Dimension Leader will build upon excellence in the predecessor leadership dimensions (particularly the trust-based Systems Leadership that creates aligned systems), shifting their primary focus from incrementally improving the performance of the organization to fundamentally changing the organizational vision, values, and culture so it can become the organization it aspires to be. Future-oriented within the context of a VUCA world...

Genuine Strategic Leadership is truly transformational by its very nature.

Strategic Leadership of this sort must be tightly focused at the top. A healthy organization cannot have multiple leaders with multiple visions leading change in multiple directions. This is not to say that there cannot be more than one Strategic Leader. Many individuals can and should strive to become Strategic Leaders within their own operating unit. However, the strategic visions at all of the lower levels must be aligned with the strategic vision at the top of the entire organization.

Strategic Leadership must be exercised very narrowly at the top, but Strategic Leadership skills can be beneficial to both Operational and Systems level leaders, and can be exercised effectively within a single department or business unit. It should be noted, though, that there is a time-allotment issue at work here. Lower levels can and should utilize strategic leadership skills, but the amount of time devoted to operations goes up the lower in the organization you go.

In the first three dimensions, primary emphasis is internally focused on executing with excellence, continuously improving current operations, and creating stable and healthy systems that ensure outstanding performance. This fourth dimension, however, shifts emphasis away from current internal operations and towards understanding, managing, and shaping an ambiguous future buffeted by constant and often dramatic change. The primary leader still bears responsibility for all that is happening within the organization, but their allocation of time and personal attention moves from what is going on "in here" to how we might respond to what is going on "out there" —

Strategic focus requires external focus.

In order to do this, the primary leader must have developed a high degree of personal competency in each of the predecessor leadership dimensions, as well as created an organization-wide leadership structure that is functioning well at each level of leadership. If the primary leader has not created a structure of underlying leadership competency at subordinate levels, her time will be taken up with solving internal operational problems created by poor leadership, rather than spending time where it should be spent: dealing with strategic issues for the future.

Strategic Leaders are concerned with where the world is headed. They're concerned with the latest demographic, economic, technological, environmental, social, and financial trends. They want to stay as current as possible with cutting edge management practices and thinking. Consequently...

A Strategic Leader places emphasis on executive learning.

This is a very different kind of learning than the kind emphasized in the predecessor levels. In earlier levels, the emphasis is on skills-based learning to achieve competency as a leader within the organization; at the Strategic Leadership level, the learning is information-based and externally-focused. The primary role of the Strategic Leader shifts from current, internal operations to identifying, assessing, interpreting, communicating about, and preparing for future conditions the organization may be facing, followed by articulation of a coherent and persuasive vision of exactly what the future should look like in practical terms. Then comes the development of a clearly achievable game plan for how to turn the vision into a reality.

An essential component of this game plan must be the development of a leadership pipeline. Any vision that fails to incorporate the logical, intentional, and effective development of leaders who are committed to the organizational culture, vision, and values is merely tactical rather than strategic in nature. It may put out today's fire, but it will not in any significant way move the organization closer to its desired future. The absence of a truly strategic approach to visioning will perpetuate a culture of institutional mediocrity and frustration. Long-term vision will fall victim to unwitting stealth incompetents masquerading as leaders.

This is not to say that the Strategic Leader must be the sole source of the vision. Depending upon the governance structure of a particular organization, the role of the Strategic Leader in developing the organization's vision will be shared to varying degrees with the governing body and other top executives. However, the Strategic Leader must be the primary driver when it comes to moving the vision from dream to reality. The Strategic Leader must also act as the primary "vision enforcer" — constantly evaluating operational systems and performance to ensure that everyone is actually moving in the right direction to achieve the desired future, allocating resources wisely so they are aligned properly as well.

With the first three dimensions, leadership development is learning to change how you do things to be more effective. At this fourth dimension, leadership development is learning to question how you think about things to more effectively shape and mold the future.

As a result, the developmental process for Strategic Leadership is quite different from the previous dimensions. Core competencies are still identified, mirroring those identified in the earlier levels, and the emphasis on continual learning is equally stressed. Leaders are readers, and exposure to big ideas in leading business books and journals broadens the horizons within which the Strategic Leader thinks about the specific future of their own organization. One way to accomplish this efficiently may be to offer Executive Book Briefings or incentivizing those who consume business literature on a regular basis.

Because the very nature of Strategic Leadership involves continuous learning, Executive Book Briefings should be provided in on ongoing cycle to create a cultural commitment to being a learning organization. The identified competencies may remain constant, but the Briefings should utilize different books in each cycle based on the current leading business literature associated with each various competency. For maximum impact, these Briefings should be cascaded down through the organization with discussion guides shared via staff meetings at all levels. This approach not only reinforces a culture of continuous learning, it also creates multiple opportunities within each operating unit to discuss current issues and trends within leadership thinking, enhancing organizational communication and performance.

Of course, serially reading hot topic books and trying to mimic the language and solutions they espouse is the classic recipe for Management by BS. Still, exposure to a wide variety of leading thinkers is critical to creating a learning organization that is open to transformation. The key to avoiding Management by BS is being willing to learn from the ideas and experiences of others and figuring out how to incorporate those lessons into your context.

07

Elements of Leadership Competency

The presupposition of 4th Dimension Leadership is that…

Great leaders are not born and cannot be trained, but they can be developed.

I'm not trying to describe the ideal leader here. Nor am I attempting to hold up select individuals as the mold from which all leaders should be cast. Instead, I'm describing a process of developing great leaders and the importance of progressively building incremental competencies in that developmental process. These competencies can all be developed, but there is a sequence to them. Following that sequence is what determines whether someone will attain their full potential as a leader or end up as a stealth incompetent, unknowingly perpetuating a culture of mediocrity.

The following Leadership Competency Elements provides a thumbnail sketch of core leadership competencies. But while the same core competencies exist for all leaders regardless of level… HOW leadership is exercised is different in each of the four dimensions. For example, Managing Change is a universal leadership competency. But for a front line employee, it may look like adapting well with a positive attitude to change that is determined by others; while for a mid-level manager it may look like designing and leading assigned change initiatives in a way that employees respond with a positive attitude and successful implementation; and for a senior executive it may look like leading cultural transformation.

One thing to remember, though, is that while the sequence of developing competency in all elements for each of the four dimensions of leadership is critically important, a leader never "moves on" to the next level of leadership. Rather than "moving on", a great leader "builds upon" the previously developed competencies and adds to their leadership toolbox. It is also important to note that while these 20 elements are core, it is not an exhaustive list of every competency every organization may want to instill in their leaders.

So, the following Leadership Competency Elements does NOT suggest that a Strategic Leader always responds to a situation by using Strategic Leadership skills. On the contrary, a Strategic Leader opens their toolbox and selects the right tool for the job at hand. Strategic Leaders can respond to a given situation relationally, operationally, systemically, or strategically, as the specific circumstances warrant.

> **Commitment to Lead:** Making the conscious commitment to lead and to practice behaviors that make effective leadership a reality, for the benefit of others.

> **Compassionate Service:** Rendering assistance motivated by genuine concern, willingly given to meet other's needs.

> **Compliance Adherence:** Facilitating adherence to laws, regulations and policies that apply to day-to-day job responsibilities; thereby limiting liability, enhancing safety, and minimizing employee wrongdoing.

> **Crisis Management:** Supporting and facilitating processes by which an organization prevents and deals with major events that threaten to harm the organization, its stakeholders, or the general public.

Customer Service Orientation: Placing customer satisfaction at the core of each decision, focused on helping customers meet their long-term needs.

Diversity and Inclusion/Citizen Care: Addressing and supporting multiple lifestyles and personal characteristics within defined groups and providing support for acceptance and respect for various geographic, cultural, racial, gender, age, socio-economic, political, and other backgrounds, being sure that all are valued, respected and supported.

Effective Decision Making: Participating in and leading effective processes for making decisions in environments marked by volatility, uncertainty, complexity and ambiguity, in a way that builds trust on the part of employees and stakeholders.

Empowerment: Embracing and facilitating autonomy and self-determination in people in order to enable them to act in a responsible and self-determined way on their own authority, overcoming powerlessness and lack of influence.

Managing Change: Supporting organizational transformation through change processes that assist others in navigating needed initiatives.

People Skills: Communicating effectively with people, in a variety of contexts, in a friendly, sincere, and effective manner.

Performance Management: Constantly improving organizational effectiveness through ongoing evaluation of systems and processes to ensure a results oriented effectiveness while maintaining a customer centric focus of all programs and services.

Personnel Management: Improving organizational effectiveness by improving the performance of employees and by developing the capabilities of teams and individual contributors.

Political Savvy: Mastering organizational and community political dynamics and avoiding forms of expression or action that are perceived to exclude, marginalize, or insult anyone... particularly groups of people who are socially disadvantaged or discriminated against.

Principle Centered Leadership: A deep commitment to do the right thing for the right reason, regardless of the circumstances.

Problem Solving/Consensus Building: Identifying problems, evaluating solutions, and decision making through analysis and selection of solutions.

Public Information and Relations: Maintaining a professional, favorable public image utilizing modern media/communications and stakeholder groups to maintain positive relations in the public's consciousness, to build a mutually beneficial relationship with the public.

Responsible Stewardship: Accepting and executing the responsibility for proper planning and management of resources with regard to the financial health of the organization, as well as the environment and nature, community economics, health, property, information, and other matters of public concern, always within a long term context.

Self-Awareness/Self-Management: Possessing emotional awareness, accurate self-assessment, and self-confidence leading to personal competence, thereby providing the opportunity to positively influence others.

Team Leadership: Providing guidance, instruction, and direction to a group of individuals for the purpose of achieving a key result or group of aligned results.

Adoption of Innovation/Technology: Providing appropriate leadership and strategies to create a culture of innovation including the adoption of new technology to stay at the leading edge.

08

Designing
4th Dimension Leadership Development Content

08

Designing
4th Dimension Leadership Development Content

Training in OWCH organizations is often simultaneously one of the most wasteful and underfunded activities imaginable. Ironically, those two opposing descriptions are directly linked to one another. Traditional training classes, with little in the way of tangible results to show for the investment of time, energy, and money, become an easy budget cut when times get tough. And yet the organizations that most need to invest in developing their people are the ones who become the most jaded by the lack of results and end up underfunding employee development.

The solution is not simply throwing more money at training. The solution is figuring out what works and what doesn't — and doing more of the former and less of the latter.

There are five hallmarks of training programs that fail. The more these describe your training environment, the less likely you will be to succeed — and, typically, the less likely you will be to have support for training in general by upper management.

The first hallmark of failed training:
Menu-Driven Training Classes

Frequently, the problem is not the quality of training being delivered. Rather, it is that the training is offered a la carte, either voluntarily selected by the trainee based on their personal interest or, worse, it gives the appearance of being remedial in nature. There is no clear scope and sequence, no rhyme or reason given for selecting this training class over that one. The classes do not build upon one another. They don't even seem to relate to one another in any coherent way. Menu-driven training programs don't lead you anywhere in particular. They may be interesting, but they are not helpful for the organization that wants to develop next-level leaders.

The second hallmark of failed training:

The Absence of Integrated Building Blocks that Cross Pollinate

How each training class builds on previous training classes, how each one cross pollinates and reinforces core messages regarding leadership values and philosophy — is essential to a learning process capable of developing a true leadership pipeline. Multiple classes by multiple presenters coming from multiple perspectives with no unifying structure, message, and methodology dramatically limits the potential for long-term leadership development.

The third hallmark of failed training:

"Do as I say, not as I do" Management Attitudes

When those in upper management require subordinates to attend training but fail to continue developing their own leadership skills, they send a mixed message. They say training is important, but their actions speak louder than their words. Their lack of integrity will inevitably become infectious.

The fourth hallmark of failing training
Inadequate Funding

When tough economic times hit, training is one of the first items to be cut — even though that is precisely when the organization most needs great leadership. I understand that a poorly-designed training program that produces lackluster results is difficult to defend, but the solution to bad training isn't no training. The solution is better training — training that is well-designed and fully integrated into the life of your organization — and that often requires better funding.

The final hallmark of failed training
Failure to Create a Values-Aligned System of Systems

Fully integrated values-aligned systems are essential to reinforce high quality leadership practices.

Everything from your hiring process to your compensation structure to the way you handle interoffice discipline all contribute to an environment that either accelerates or slows down the leadership development process. Later we'll discuss in more detail some accelerators for your leadership pipeline, but training programs that falter are often training programs that never get around to instilling core values in their leadership candidates. Without it, the process slows to a crawl.

4th Dimension Leadership is designed to be a comprehensive leadership development system of systems with a fully integrated focus on values. Traditional training programs are failing at an alarming rate, particularly in their ability to have a long term, meaningful, and measurable impact on developing effective leaders at every level of an organization. The specific curricula content may vary from organization to organization as well as by level of the organization, but the 20 core elements will likely remain constant.

4TH Dimension Leaders should develop all 20 of the leadership competencies discussed in the previous section regardless of their role in the organization, but to be applied appropriately for their level of responsibility and context.

My whole point has been that it's all about leadership at every level of the organization, but the appropriate application of leadership principles varies by context and level of responsibility. For example, every employee is expected to be competent in change management appropriate to their role and level of responsibility.

At the relational level, change management looks like handling disruption with a positive attitude and sharing optimism. At the operational level, it looks like being able to inspire your team to execute well on the changes and to understand why they're important. At the systems level, it looks like carefully designed and thoughtfully planned change initiatives that build trust and confidence in the changes themselves. At the strategic level, it is both about seeing and defining what changes need to occur and creating the organizational structure that builds support for and embraces the change.

In addition to the 4th Dimension Leadership Development system, there are also three types of predecessor competencies which are essential to success. They're distinct from the leadership development content, but they are no less essential. These are personal, technical, and professional competency. Specific training in these three areas will vary widely by personality and position.

It's also important to note that there are several key questions which can be used to evaluate any leadership development program's potential for real impact. The best questions I know would be asking whether or not your program is:

- Noble — does it recognize and honor servant leadership as a true calling?

- Holistic — does it address both the professional and personal development needed to succeed?

- Challenging — does it teach genuine humility, thoughtfulness, and a hunger to learn and grow?

- Thorough — does it cover all the major aspects and competencies of leadership?

- Honest — does it operate in the realm of reality?

- Collaborative — does it encourage participants to learn from a variety of people and sources?

- Reformational — does it inspire and foster the desire to make things better?

- Hands On — does it engage in real-life problem solving?

- Rigorous — does it require time and emotional investment from the participants?

- Comprehensive — does it address all four of the leadership dimensions?

- Integrated — does each course of study build on previous learning foundations?

- Ethical — does it align with and advance your organization's core values?

The 4th Dimension Leadership model integrates the Unifying Principles, Predecessor Competencies, and Leadership Competency Elements I've described with a Servant Leadership Philosophy to help you create a cost-effective and long-term system for developing your rising generation of leaders, moving your organization towards authentic and sustainable transformation.

09

Cultural Transformation **Accelerators**

Creating a culture shift that actually sticks usually takes about three to five years and a significant investment in employee training and development — especially at mid-management levels. Typically, this change initiative is launched with great confidence by the strategic leader. The more confidence she has, the more enthusiasm front line employees exhibit (even if they may be skeptical about just how real this change is going to be and how long it's going to last). The excitement levels are usually highest at the top and bottom of the organization, with support declining the closer you get to the middle of the org chart.

Leading a true cultural transformation demands a specific Strategic Leadership skill set, and a wholehearted commitment to clear, consistent, and frequent communication. Go back and read those three adjectives: clear, consistent, and frequent. Compromise on any one of those, and you'll fail in your attempts to create lasting change. If your organization is going to "walk the talk" it needs to hear its mission, vision, and values time and time again. In fact, about the time you're tired of saying the same thing over and over, that's likely to be the first time they've heard you.

Middle Manager: "What is this Servant Leadership thing, and where can I learn more about it?"

You: "Well, you could look it up online. Or you could look at all the memos I've sent you for the past six months."

Middle Manager: "Why am I just now hearing about it?"

You: <facepalm>

You might not like this, but if you aren't a little tired of repeating yourself, you're probably not saying it often enough. Don't be discouraged. Keep saying it. Say it until you are blue in the face. Say it until you've got it memorized. Say it until you could say it in your sleep. Say it until you are tired of hearing yourself and you think that if you have to say it one more time you might just throw up, and then say it again. Be clear. Use the same language, the same words. Say it every opportunity you get, even if you think it feels forced. Clear. Consistent. Frequent. This is necessary to imprint upon all your employees the mission, the vision, and the values of your organization, as well as the desired cultural and attitudinal attributes.

Only then can a leader create a widespread understanding of what types of behaviors and attitudes are consistent with the desired culture. Once this is established, re-engineering of performance management systems can ensure that behavioral incentives and penalties are consistent with and reinforce the intended cultural environment. Success in creating a cultural shift like this is largely dependent upon the following factors:

- The extent to which the organization trusts that top executives are truly committed to their stated values and are emotionally engaged in leading the effort.

- The extent to which leaders have been selected who have high credibility as the kind of leader who could actually pull this off.

- The extent to which the effort is viewed as long-term rather than one more Management by BS flavor of the month.

- The extent to which resources are devoted to communication and training at every level of the organization.

- The extent to which employees understand what is changing, where this is headed, and why it is necessary.

- The extent to which a game plan is implemented which has measurable and visible markers of progress, but which is not so rapid as to induce anxiety.

- The extent to which middle management buys in by walking the talk.

- The extent to which executives are willing to change current operating systems, eliminate mixed messages, and align systems with the desired values and culture.

Many organizations do well on all but the last item. They devote lots of time, money, and energy to getting ready for change…but then they experience a failure of nerve when it comes time to actually alter the systems that are currently operational.

Creating a values aligned system of systems is the thing that makes cultural change real and sustainable.

10

Creating a Values Aligned System of Systems

Ultimately, it doesn't matter what your stated values are. Anyone can claim to value honesty or innovation. If your systems aren't aligned in a way that actually reinforces those values, you're lying to yourself and your employees. Your culture will never become authentic, things will always feel slightly forced, people will be insecure, and trust will not be present. It is not hyperbole to say that every effort should be made to ensure that all systems are aligned with your desired cultural values.

However, it is also true that not all systems carry equal weight. So, there are a few systems that play a particularly critical role in leadership development. If these systems are properly aligned, they will dramatically accelerate a successful and sustainable cultural transformation.

EMPLOYEE OWNERSHIP OF ORGANIZATIONAL CULTURE, VALUES AND VISIOIN

Leaders do not often respond well to being told what to do and how to do it; leaders want to be involved in those decisions. Leaders want to have a hand in shaping the culture of their workplace, helping to determine why they do what they do the way they do it. Allowing everyone to help codify your cultural values and vision goes a long way towards showing them you mean to treat them with dignity and respect, like leaders.

If you intend to create an organization of leaders, you must begin to treat your employees as such sooner rather than later.

Business Values Workshops

These workshops being the process of cultural transformation by engaging the entire organization in open and honest conversations about three key questions:

> *Q* 1. **What are our current stated values?**
> *Q* 2. **How well are we walking the talk of those values?**
> *Q* 3. **What should our authentic values be?**

These three questions provide a pivotal opportunity to evaluate whether or not the organization even knows what the currently stated values are (hint: most do not). If they are able to articulate them, it offers leadership a chance to hear from employees their perceptions of how well what is written on the walls is being lived out in the halls (hint: mostly not very well). Finally, these conversations offer employees a sense of ownership in the process of codifying a new set of values as part of the overall cultural transformation (hint: employees will usually embrace the essence of the current stated values but this gives them a chance to add their language and renew their expectation of authentic commitment to the newly stated values by the organization).

Yes, it's probably simpler for management to do this behind closed doors and then "share" them with the employees. But simple isn't always effective. The process of this is as important as the product. Allowing employees to work on crafting the statements themselves can give insight into the kind of culture they're likely to be highly engaged in. This isn't about coercion or compliance. This is about creating a culture in which your employees will thrive. That may take some extra time and effort on the front end, but it will pay dividends in the end.

When Greenleaf was writing about Servant Leadership, he proposed three questions that could be used to evaluate your commitment to his philosophy:

Q 1. Are the people we're serving being treated with dignity and respect as human beings?

Q 2. Are the people we're serving becoming more empowered, more knowledgeable, freer, and more likely, themselves, to choose to be servant leaders?

Q 3. Are the weakest among us being helped by our service, or at the very least, not further deprived?

Allowing your employees a space for unfiltered dialogue, giving them a seat at the table where your cultural values will be codified, asking them to help you in the process — that answers "Yes" to all three of Greenleaf's questions, and demonstrates just how seriously you take the entire Servant Leadership philosophy.

You should come out of this workshop with a wide ranging set of organizational values that the organization believes in although still loosely organized and not fully refined. Each workshop, depending upon the number of people involved, should last from three to four hours. The result will be a set of priority values that the Management Team can begin to consider immediately.

The Management Team will then take the reports from the organization-wide meetings and refine them so that a set of values that employees feel ownership of can be formally adopted. But more than that, you will get a better picture of where your employees are in terms of their aspirations, their disappointments, and their frustrations. The discussions may be sharp and difficult to hear, but, handled properly, this should demonstrate your willingness to listen, your desire to "Seek first to understand, then to be understood", and your commitment to treat your employees with dignity and respect — all qualities of authentic Servant Leadership.

If you show them that you're serious about being a Servant Leader, you will gain more credibility in your attempts to create a Servant Leadership culture.

Communicating the Values and Culture

Once you've figured out your values statements and the kind of culture you want, you must communicate all of that in a way that creates excitement, emotional buy-in, and a sense of pride. Involving employees in the process will help. They should feel a sense of ownership, and the final product should be a cause for celebration. But how you unveil the finished product is extremely important.

One option is to hold a series of meetings to "reveal" the work employees have done. You'd want to use video and as much creativity as possible. You'd also want to give special recognition to the people who helped craft and wordsmith the final statements. And you'd want to make sure you give senior executives the chance (and the expectation) to verbalize their commitment to walking the talk of these new statements.

The video you end up creating for this could also be used to recruit new employees and as part of their on-ramping process. Annual events like Christmas parties or picnics should always be seen as key opportunities to put the spotlight on new and creative ways to communicate your values.

Envisioning a Servant Leadership Culture Workshops

Solomon said, "There is nothing new under the sun," and that is certainly true when it comes to leadership. One of the reasons Servant Leadership endures, despite more than half a century's worth of Management by BS trends which hit the bestseller list and then fade into the twilight, is that Greenleaf tapped into a set of universally noble ideals which address some of our deepest yearnings. These qualities transcend time and fashion. These are traits we all hunger for in our leaders!

Servant Leadership captures the radical sense of constructive tension I discussed in the beginning. A radical leader returns to the roots of healthy relationships with her followers while also challenging those followers to join together in the journey beyond their comfort zones, to explore the leading edge of possibility.

We all want a leader who will simultaneously make us feel safe and cared for but also bold and daring.

Servant Leaders are constantly pushing the boundaries, testing, assessing, and recalibrating ideas of what is doable to strike a perfect balance between security and adventure. That constructive tension of radical leaders creates a culture of consistent transformation required to thrive in a VUCA world.

Greenleaf's Servant Leadership philosophy taps into our deep yearnings for traits we all want in our leaders. Anytime you engage your employees in honest conversation about Business Values they want to see lived out in your organization, you're going to hear Servant Leadership language. Your people may express it in different words and phrases, but it will always come back to the same thing — we want our leaders to be servants, and we want to present ourselves as Servant Leaders.

Your cultural transformation truly begins when all employees start answering the three questions in the Business Values Workshops and reach consensus on a list of values the organization aspires to. Presuming those values are consistent with a Servant Leadership culture (and they will be if you have a truly open and authentic conversation with your employees), next comes a series of workshops in which the management team can explicitly understand the implications of Servant Leadership and are given the chance to think through what it would look like if this became the leadership philosophy that binds together all of the operating systems of their organization in real and practical terms.

Envisioning a Servant Leadership Culture Workshops

The format for these workshops is simple. But unlike the Business Values workshops which involve every employee, these workshops are designed for the Management Team to engage in deeper discussions about how to actually implement the values in the specific operational processes of various systems described in this chapter.

Start by presenting the core values that the organization has adopted (and that the employees as a whole now own). Then present the basics of Servant Leadership including the importance of a creating a system of value aligned systems if you are going to make the culture authentic. This workshop is typically most effective with a two day schedule.

The first half day is devoted to "what is Servant Leadership and Why Does It Matter to Us?" The second half day is devoted both to effective team building and to the concepts of building a system of systems. The second day goes deep on each of the particular systems and specific strategies for aligning them with the values.

In the day two session, divide everyone up into groups of three to discuss one of the systems (as detailed in this chapter on creating a system of systems). Have all groups discuss how to create an authentic servant leadership culture that is aligned with your organization's uniquely described values with regard to that specific system for about 20 minutes. Typically there are three questions to be explored in each small group:

Q1. What is really working well with this system?
Q2. What is not working so well with this system?

*Q*3. What improvements would take this system to a higher performance level and ensure alignment with and reinforcement of our agreed upon values and the principles of a Servant Leadership culture?

After each system is discussed, have each group summarize the key ideas from their discussion for the large group and record them on chart paper. At this stage, it is about proliferation of ideas not refinement of the ideas. After each group reports in, have everyone get into different small groups to discuss the same three questions for the next system to be considered.

This will produce wide ranging strategies that you can begin exploring to create an organizational culture that authentically walks the talk. Teams should be assigned responsibility for focusing on each of the various systems. They should be tasked with evaluating and refining all of the options and ideas from the workshop and recommending which specific strategies should be implemented.

In other words, there is a three-step process: (1) Organization-wide employee meetings on Business Values to receive input and feedback on what the organization's desired values are followed by a management team workshop to absorb and synthesize employee input and formally adopt a set of core values; (2) A management team workshop on Envisioning a Servant Leadership Culture to fully understand Servant Leadership and identify specific ideas and strategies for creating aligned systems; (3) Strike force meetings centered around each system to develop action plans to make walking the talk a sustainable reality.

EMPLOYEE RECRUITMENT AND SELECTION

The process of developing new leaders begins even before you hire an individual.

It begins by taking steps to create a large pool of high-quality candidates who are aligned with your organizational values. This is true even in the case of front line employees. Most of your future leaders will start on the front lines. Hire well at those positions, and your leadership pipeline is ahead of most organizations.

Okay, so odds are most future leaders do not currently start on your front lines...but they should! If you implement the process we're discussing here, you'll dramatically increase the number of internal promotions rather than having to recruit leaders from outside of your organization. When you must venture outside of your current employee base, that hiring process should be a great one, too, but you want to be able to promote from within because you hired so well from the start.

A 4th Dimension Leadership recruitment process communicates culture and values even before it offers a job description. It matters little how fast they can type or whether or not they've mastered Excel spreadsheets if they are not a good fit for your organizational culture. If they do not fit your values, they do not fit your organization, and you must assist them in self-selecting out if they're not aligned with the culture you seek to create. The quality of your recruitment documents and advertising influences the quality of candidates who apply. Don't skimp here.

Outstanding prospective employees usually have options. You're going to be competing with some of the greatest recruiting minds out there. If your process is unprofessional or unattractive, if you don't communicate well with the candidate, if your process feels awkward, slow, or frustrating, you will lose the best candidates. That means you'll end up with the mediocre candidates who stay in the hunt because they have fewer options.

That is not to say that you cannot help mediocre candidates become excellent leaders. However, it will take more time, energy, and resources to do so. You're giving your competitors a head start by allowing your recruitment process to be run in a way that discourages outstanding candidates, lowering the quality of the prospect pool.

Organizational Brand and Reputation Management

Every single day 10,000 Baby Boomers turn 65. The number of Baby Boomers reaching retirement age is greater than the number of next generation employees prepared to step up and take their place. That means the number of jobs available will soon eclipse the number of excellent available candidates. Your organization is going to have to get better at selling your organizational "brand" to prospective employees if you want to compete for the best and brightest. Your reputation will profoundly influence the quality of applicants you see. Becoming known as an organization of integrity, a place where the ideals of Servant Leadership aren't just given lip-service but are actually lived out, gives you a competitive advantage as the next generation makes organizational culture a priority consideration.

Of course, brand management does not happen on its own. Or, rather, *good* brand management does not happen that way. You must develop a specific set of strategies to do so.

Talent Marketing Collateral Materials

Mediocre marketing materials attract mediocre candidates. Dynamic and well-written job announcements, visually attractive brochures, easy-to-navigate websites where potential employees can learn about your organization and employment opportunities — these are all significant factors in recruiting the best of the next generation. It may even be wise to invest in a professional writer and a professional graphic designer.

This is not just about conveying information about the position; the materials themselves convey your organization's overall commitment to excellence. The medium is part of your message. This is also an opportunity for you to explicitly state your organizational values and alert candidates that if they're not aligned with those values they'd be better off looking for employment elsewhere. Introducing the concept of Servant Leadership here allows for an easier conversation about it in the interview process.

Social Media Talent Marketing

Social Media is here to stay, and it is rapidly replacing traditional advertising venues as the way to reach the best prospects. At a bare minimum, your organization should utilize Linked In, Twitter, and Facebook accounts to link candidates to a professionally developed position profile brochure on your company's website. And increasingly, Instagram and Pinterest are gaining momentum in talent recruitment. Again, you must make sure that your Social Media account, website, and brochure all reveal your commitment to excellence as well as your core values. Each Social Media platform requires a different style of writing, graphical presentations, interaction, and timing. A failure to understand the differences and execute a proper strategy can end up sending the opposite message of what you intend.

Do it right, or don't do it at all.

Candidate Screening Processes

Maybe the most consistent weakness in the entire hiring process is the failure to consider the future leadership potential of entry level employees. I understand. You need to fill a position. Sometimes that can feel urgent. But if you hire in a hurry you'll end up settling for "good enough" and perpetuate a culture of mediocre talent - people who are not aligned with your organizational values. And, not to sound like a broken record here, but it really is about leadership at every level of the organization — leadership exercised appropriately for the context.

I recently read that you have a 14% chance of making a great hire if you use traditional interview techniques. The article went on to say that you have a 17% chance of making a great hire if you put all the applicants' names into a hat and randomly draw one. I'm not sure if that's true, but it seems right from my experience. The typical interview process does not produce the results we want, and yet we continue doing the same thing over and over again, hoping for better results this time. That, of course, is the definition of insanity.

Over the years I've developed four guideposts that I believe dramatically improve the hiring process. Combining this with a long-term leadership development perspective should increase the odds of you making a great hire.

The first guidepost:

The best predictor of future performance is past performance.

I know there are some who disagree on this, given the near-constant fluctuations of living in a VUCA world, but hear me out. I may not mean what you think I mean when I say this.

According to Claudio Fernandez-Araoz, a leading executive search practitioner for more than 25 years and best-selling author, a candidate's behavior may change, but their motivation probably won't. He says if someone is driven purely by selfish motives this is likely to remain consistent. Other qualities that are near-constant would be curiosity, insight, engagement, and determination. Scour a candidate's background for these things — not simply a specific set of skills and competencies. Look beyond their professional history to uncover stories that reveal something about their character. Do what you must to discover whether the person has (or lacks) these qualities.

The second guidepost:

The prospect is the very best they will ever be in their pursuit of this position.

Fernadez-Araoz jokingly refers to most job interviews as a conversation between two liars. Both sides are working overtime to present themselves at their best. The interviewer is probably going to present the organization in its best light, covering over flaws and pretending the organization is healthier than it actually is. The candidate is doing the same thing about herself. This may or may not be an attempt to deceive. It may just be that we see things as we want them to be, ourselves included. Optimistic people tend to overrate their own performance and potential. Still, it is vital for you to remember this: the candidate is presenting their highlight reel; don't expect them to be better on the job than they are in the hiring process.

If they submit a resume with spelling mistakes in it, their work product will probably be error-laden. If they are late to the appointment, they will probably have time-management issues once hired. If they are socially awkward in the interview process, they will be socially awkward in the office. If their email address is something like drinkyouunderthetable@yahoo.com or ihackicloudaccounts@gmail.com — you should know what you're in for.

The third guidepost:

Employees are generally hired for aptitude but fired for attitude.

Technical skills, IQ, past performance at meeting work-related objectives — these things are fairly easy to assess. Consequently, few people who do not have the technical skills to do a job get hired. However, attitude and personality attributes are harder to assess. Some employers just shrug and take the easy road of not even trying. I cannot overstate how shortsighted this is.

There are a number of inexpensive tools that offer insight into behavioral patterns, attitudes, and approaches to interpersonal relationships. Failing to invest in these tools may be penny wise, but it's pound foolish. One bad attitude employee can cost you far more to fire (and hire their replacement) than you'll spend on assessment tools. Be wise on the front end, and you're less likely to regret it later.

The fourth guidepost:

If you don't believe you have a great candidate, don't hire.

The most common mistake I see in this entire process is hiring someone you're not really excited about. I understand. You're in a hurry, and the idea of starting over seems daunting. Slow down. Take your time. Make a great decision, and if you don't have a great option...don't settle.

Various employee selection systems have been developed over time to improve your odds of hiring a rock star instead of settling for a one-hit wonder.

Candidate Screening for Role Fit

A resume can demonstrate whether or not a candidate is *qualified* for a certain role; a psychometric assessment considers how *suitable* a candidate is for that position. Using such assessments has been linked to a significant increase in the rate of success over using traditional techniques — mostly because these tools help identify the developmental strengths and weaknesses of a candidate, which allows you to be more effective in addressing training needs.

For example, people who provide outstanding customer service tend to score highly on attributes such as listening skills, empathy, and overall likability. Imagine two candidates who have similar qualifications; their resumes are nearly identical. One has the behavioral profile for great customer service, while the other has a behavior profile that customers are likely to find off-putting. One of these candidates will make the organization look great; the other will damage credibility and relationships.

On the other hand, those same two candidates may actually be reversed if the job has to do with handling internal disputes and compliance with governmental regulations. The person who customers want to interact with may be completely inept at mediating conflicts and working towards a peaceful resolution, while the one with the "off-putting" personality may be able to function incredibly well when it comes to ensuring overall compliance and cooperation among co-workers.

Two employees — equally valuable to your organization provided they are each in the right position. Both outcomes are predictable…if you use the right tools to make such a prediction.

Mitchell Kusy and Elizabeth Holloway have written insightfully about this in their book *Toxic Workplace*. They write: "When you interview potential team members, how much time do you spend trying to determine the applicant's fit within the team? Typically leaders spend an inordinate amount of time on the content of the team's work — such factors as expertise, education, and work on similar projects. We are not saying these aren't important. What we are saying is that you need to spend time on more subtle personality factors when recruiting individuals and team members."

Organizations waste tremendous amounts of money on bad hires, because they refuse to invest relatively small amounts of money on doing a better job assessing candidates before they are hired. We're asking candidates the wrong questions, so their answers aren't helping us determine whether or not they will be a great long-term fit for this particular role. They may be a great person, but they may not be the best person for this position.

Candidate Screening for Team Fit

It's not enough to evaluate how suitable a candidate is for a particular role; you must also evaluate how well a candidate will match the team they'll be joining. Bill Hybels, the founding and senior pastor of Willow Creek Community Church, one of the largest churches in North America, says he always examines a candidate's character first, then he looks at competency, but before he hires someone he considers chemistry. Will this person fit in with everyone else?

It's not uncommon in the world of sports to see a team win a world championship, even if they are not as talented as some of the other teams in contention. One of the determining factors of success is overall team chemistry. Do the team members get along with one another? Do they work together and have fun while getting things done? Is there a sense of camaraderie and mutual respect? These factors can help a team that has fewer superstars compete and succeed.

There are tools out there that can help you determine how a potential team member will interact with his new teammates. A dramatic change agent and a steady maintainer may look identical on paper, but how they interact with their team will be as different as can be. One behavioral style is not necessarily better than the other, but one will definitely be a better fit for this team. Both styles are highly predictable, again, if you have the right tools at your disposal.

Candidate Screening for Eligibility

This part of the process examines whether or not a candidate can actually get the job done. There's the role, there's the team, and then there's the task. Your goal is to select a finalist group who fit the role, fit the team, and are qualified to do the job. To use Hybels' three Cs: you want candidates who fit the role (Character), fit the team (Chemistry), and can do the job (Competency). Settling for mediocrity in any of these areas will spell disaster for your organization's future.

Stage 1 of the screening process for eligibility is a questionnaire asking approximately 10 basic questions regarding qualifications. You might ask, "How did you learn to do this?" You might ask, "How long have you been doing this?" You might ask, "What parts of this do you find most challenging, and which parts are most rewarding?" This is to discover a candidate's level of experience. Do they have the right certifications (a CPA, for example)? Do they have the right education (a Bachelor's degree, for example)? Do they have an adequate track record (5 years experience as a heavy equipment operator, for example)? This is the most basic screening level stuff that should be included in a resume, but it targets specific requirements to screen out those who are fundamentally unqualified. The point of this initial questionnaire is to quickly weed out those who do not have the requisite qualifications to do the job.

The second part of eligibility screening is a resume review. This is your chance to go deeper with the candidate. The first questionnaire eliminates those who do not meet basic qualifications, while the resume review begins to evaluate candidates alongside one another to determine which ones warrant continuing in the process based on experience and track record.

Once you've narrowed the field to a group of 10-12 carefully considered semi-finalists your odds of making a great hire rise dramatically. You've chosen individuals who have an impressive track record, who meet qualifications, and who have a high predictability of fit for both the role and the team. Now it's time for the candidate vetting phase.

Written Questionnaire Vetting

A written questionnaire can provide insights into the communication skills, the thought processes, and the leadership philosophy of the semi-finalists. This insight is invaluable in terms of evaluating alignment and predicting success. If there's some specialized experience you're looking for, something that may not show up on a standard resume, this is a great time to explore that.

For example, a CPA may have been a requirement for this position, but if forensic accounting experience is what you really want (even if it's not a "requirement"), the questionnaire would be an appropriate way to question specific experience in special issues. The ways in which candidates answer questions like these give you greater insight into the kind of person they are and the kind of employee they are likely to be. They'll reveal their understanding of relationships, core values, and leadership much more through stories than just through a one dimensional finalist interview.

One other consideration that lends itself to placing a high value on written questionnaires: some people are naturally good at speaking off-the-cuff. Others need time to think and consider their responses. Neither of these is better than the other. One may be better for a particular role, but some of the greatest leaders in the world aren't always the best at speaking spontaneously. Given the chance to ponder and craft a response, though, they may surprise you.

Online Recorded Interview

An online recorded interview can provide additional insights into a candidate's technological literacy, verbal communication skills, and enthusiasm for the position. These will typically include 4-5 questions with a maximum response time of 5 minutes each. You might ask, "Why do you want to work for this organization?" You might ask, "What excites you about possibly getting this job?" You might ask, "What can you offer our organization that you believe would make you a great hire?"

All of the information compiled so far should be utilized to narrow the field to a smaller group of 4-6 finalists to be invited in for personal interviews.

There are four distinct areas required to effectively vet your final candidates: (1) comprehensive media searches (including social media); (2) legal/civil/criminal background checks; (3) reference checks; (4) the face-to-face interview process. The first three are primarily about avoiding any surprises. The fourth step, if all of the prior steps have been taken, is predominantly about assessing chemistry and cultural values alignment.

Comprehensive Media Searches

No media search should ever determine your hiring decision in and of itself. However, a media search can provide insight and understanding into the values of the candidate. There may be some issues you want to explore as a result of your findings. This search should obviously include mainstream publications such as newspapers, but also social media sites and internet search engines. The last thing you want is for some critic to dig up some dirt on one of your new hires, dirt that was available to you if you'd only done a thorough enough search.

Now, there are some legal issues you should be aware of. You can review an applicant's public postings and accounts, but be careful. Once you see all that stuff, you're also seeing things like gender, race, religion, and sexual orientation. Those are "protected characteristics" the court will assume you are now aware of.

If you choose to review social media as part of your hiring practices, some say it's probably best to wait until after you've met the candidate face to face. Their reasoning is you're less likely to be accused of making your decision based on those protected characteristics you discovered through a social network profile. However, those media searches will also help prepare you for the face-to-face meetings. The concerns about protected classes may not be paramount if this is only done after you've selected the group you are going to interview. Laws pertaining to social media are continuing to evolve. Checking in with an attorney familiar with employment issues, privacy, and the changing laws regarding social media can help keep you out of hot water. It's not entirely clear what a potential employer can legally do with a candidate who slams his current boss on a social media site, but you can create a social media policy as part of your organization's social media strategy.

Regardless, if you're going to use social media in this process, make sure you're consistent. Conduct the same searches at the same point in the process for every applicant. And use some common sense. If you do find something that makes you wonder about a candidate's judgment or professionalism, be sure to print or save screen shots.

As for other negative information you may turn up — pictures of the candidate getting drunk, making ignorant or bigoted comments, or just doing something stupid — treat that the same way you would if you discovered that information in the interview or from a reference.

Background Checks (legal/civil/criminal)

Many organizations use background check mills who buy massive data dumps and repackage them. That's an inexpensive way to say you've done a background check, but it leaves you at risk for undiscovered issues. Depending upon how your background checks are conducted, you are required to have a legal release form completed by the applicant, informing that person of his or her rights, and providing that applicant with a copy of the report. The rules will vary based on federal, state, local, and job-specific laws. Check with an attorney if you're unsure of how to proceed.

As with your social media searches, make sure that the process for all applicants is consistent. Different positions may require different levels of investigation, but try to make the process as uniform as possible to avoid any charges of discrimination. Besides, the process is more effective if it's consistent. You cannot compare apples to apples if you're using different processes. Using a highly specific and defined protocol for social media background as well as legal/civil/criminal searches is a must.

If you find something troublesome that may impact your decision to hire an applicant, it can be wise to engage in a personal conversation with that applicant. Mistakes, reporting errors, and miscommunications are always possible, and many of them can be resolved with a simple face-to-face conversation.

Look for patterns. One bad day in her 20s shouldn't determine a candidate's employability for the rest of her life. We've all made mistakes, and everyone deserves a second chance. Considering consistent patterns of job relevant behavior — positive or negative — is a defensible way for employers to make hiring decisions.

Reference Checks

By this stage of the process, you should know whether or not the candidate in question is qualified to do the job. Reference checks are primarily about character, integrity, leadership style, and behavioral issues. It's always best to provide a list of people by position who you want to talk to rather than relying on the candidate to tell you who they want you to talk to. You probably want to utilize an interviewer who is experienced at doing reference checks and has a series of questions that will explore values and behavior to evaluate cultural alignment.

If all you ask are the usual questions like "Was he a good team player?" or "On a scale of 1-10 how would you rate her integrity?" — well, you're not going to learn much. Think back to the core skills needed for this job and the competencies needed for this role. Think about the core values you want embodied. Ask questions related to that stuff.

If, during your interview, you asked the candidate about communication, decision-making, and time management, ask the reference the same questions. "Tell me about a time when she had a problem with a co-worker. How did she handle it?" Or, "Can you give me an example of a time when he had to make a quick decision. How did he think that through, and how did he communicate it to you?"

The questions you ask should prompt the candidate's references to talk about the candidate's past behavior and thought process. You can't do that in a two-minute phone call or in a few lines of an email. You'll learn the other stuff — about being a team player and having integrity — but you'll also learn a lot more than that…if you ask the right questions.

One last question you might want to consider — and this is the only hypothetical question you should ever ask in a reference check — is, "Would you ever hire him again?" The answer to this question will tell you a lot more than asking about sick days and tardiness. After all, there's a huge difference between, "Uh…yeah…I think so," and, "Absolutely, in a heartbeat."

Oh, and make sure you let them answer the questions without you putting words in their mouth. Don't say things like, "What you're saying is that he is a real team player, right?" Or, "Maybe she just didn't like the management style over there.

Sounds like we run things very differently here. I bet she'll fit in just fine."

Ask thoughtful and thought-provoking questions, and then let them answer the questions you've asked. Listen. Take notes. Process this well. A bad hire can cost you between one and five times the annual salary of the position. You don't want to spend that money if you could avoid it by taking your time in the hiring process.

Behavioral Interviewing Techniques

When it comes to the final interview, it's wise to use a team interview panel. We don't like to admit it, but too many good candidates get sent packing because we think they're too tall or too short, too thin or too husky, we don't like the look of them, or maybe they just remind us too much of our former spouse. Having a team prevents those kinds of biases from hindering our hiring process.

Also, make sure to use behavioral interviewing techniques, questions that aim at learning about past behaviors in specific work situations. You're looking to hire someone who will behave in a way that is aligned with your stated core values and Servant Leader attitudes. Ask questions that will reveal whether or not this candidate has demonstrated that kind of behavior in the past. If you're looking to hire a leader, ask them to tell you about a time when they took the lead on a difficult project.

Common behavior-based question categories include teamwork, problem solving, initiative/leadership, interpersonal skills, and dealing with stress, pressure, or high-challenge assignments. If you prepare questions to cover each of these five categories, you'll cover your bases pretty well.

These types of questions are trying to find out how the candidate behaved in the past in order to predict how they will behave in the future. They reveal a candidate's core values (which are often only truly revealed under pressure). They tell you about their understanding of leadership. This is invaluable information you aren't likely to get from a resume, background check, or references.

EMPLOYEE ONBOARDING

So, you've made the hire and your new rock star employee is ready to join the team. Do you have an on-ramping process that will clearly communicate your organizational DNA, your core values and behavioral/performance expectations? Does your on-ramping process help a new hire develop a career path so you can optimize your training and development investments in them?

Every new hire needs to hear more than procedures, policies, and processes; they need to hear the vision, mission, and values of your organization in an inspirational and empowering way. The on-ramping process must include stated values, expectations, accountability measures, and practical insights into what a Servant Leadership culture looks like in daily practice.

Most candidates are going to have heard similar language from multiple organizations. This is your chance to show them that you fully intend to walk the talk and that you expect the same from them in return. This is the only way to effectively communicate what the new hire can expect from others and what others expect from the new hire.

A process that has formal touch points at initial employment and again at 30, 60, 90 days and at 1 year will provide the organizational discipline to ensure quality communications take place as the new hire grows into her new role. Incorporating "skip level" meetings into these touch points can communicate that the employee is valuable and that the organization is investing in them and committed to their long-term growth.

DEVELOPING YOUR PEOPLE

There is no single duty more critical for a leader than to inspire people to want to be their best — and then wisely investing in their development so they can achieve their potential. As we discussed earlier, 4th Dimension Leadership acknowledges that leadership is not something done from the top down. Rather, the most dynamic organizations are those who understand that leadership occurs on every level. It is applied in contextually-appropriate ways for each person's role and level of responsibility, but leadership happens in every department, in every division, on every floor, at every level of the organizational chart.

Investing in the development of your people to help them reach their full potential is at the very heart of Servant Leadership.

It is also the only way to thrive in a VUCA world.

A coherent leadership developmental process can also help the entire chain of command do a better job of developing their people. OWCH organizations expect managers and supervisors to train their employees but do little or nothing to equip them to do so with excellence. Poorly equipped managers and supervisors often create a higher level of anxiety and a lower level of performance because of their inability to differentiate between performance issues and development opportunities.

Both need to be addressed, but if they're not addressed effectively (as part of a comprehensive development program) it can be counter-productive.

As we saw earlier, there are some basic performance-based competencies required to do the job well: Personal Competencies; Technological Competencies; and Professional Competencies. These are the foundational skills and attributes an employee must possess before they can develop into a leader.

It's a given that your organization must try to hire people who already have these competencies. With them as a baseline, however, you'll still need a solid developmental process that fosters and reinforces a leadership culture. Every leader must know what is expected of them behaviorally and that they will be held accountable for walking the talk of the Business Values and Servant Leadership philosophy.

The question is not how to turn your employees into leaders. Everyone at every level of your organization is a leader already. The question is whether or not your organization is willing to create the type of aligned systems that will help those leaders exercise the right competencies and skill sets for their role. This is how good organization achieve greatness. They don't necessarily create better leaders; they create better systems in which the leaders they have can learn, grow, and thrive. OWCH organizations maintain the status quo and nurture mediocrity by relying on leadership development by osmosis and rigid structures that actually discourage employees from seeing themselves as leaders.

If your organization is going to live out what it claims to value and believe, these principles cannot be left behind after the initial orientation process is completed. They must permeate the entire culture of your organization. Every office, every hallway, every conference room, every break room must exude enthusiasm for these principles. Leadership training and development courses must be regularly scheduled to consistently reinforce behavioral expectations. Every class offered by the organization should be scrutinized to ensure that it is philosophically consistent with your Business Values and a Servant Leadership culture. Not only will this cross pollination help you walk the talk, it will prevent the tendency OWCH organizations have of sending mixed messages about values and behavior.

One other thing to consider: given the technology bias among younger employees, your development program should include both live and online content delivery strategies. A blended learning environment is essential these days for optimal impact. Older employees may be more receptive to live training and more resistant to online. Younger employees may reverse that. The reality is that both groups benefit by being forced to leave their comfort zones and utilize a variety of learning methods. It doesn't hurt that online learning is more affordable than live learning, but more and more studies are showing that there are still some things that are best taught in a live room with a live instructor.

Performance Evaluations

Can we be honest and admit that what have been traditionally called "Annual Performance Reviews" are largely ineffective? According to an article by Dori Meinert in the Society for

Human Resource Management's *HR Magazine* from April, 2015, 95% of employees are dissatisfied with their company's appraisal process and 90% don't believe the process provides accurate information. Approximately 65% say that the current performance appraisal process interferes with their productivity and offers irrelevant information.

Rooted in the 20th Century view of employees as easily replaceable cogs in the business wheel, these have devolved into little more than an easily manipulated process wherein a supervisor arbitrarily gives a subordinate the pay raise they believe is necessary to keep the cog quietly in place for another year. It's outdated, ineffective, and — if we're being completely honest — kind of insulting.

Today's leaders must do more than simply complete the documentation required by HR. They must seek to understand each employee's skill and morale levels. The Servant Leader's role is to unlock an employee's potential and help her achieve her goals, to help her become a better version of who she is. Servant Leaders understand that, rather than trying to control people, they have a responsibility to care for them by coaching them.

Ongoing performance coaching can take place in short conversations held weekly, monthly, or quarterly. This allows the leader to check on the morale of employees and understand their level of engagement. It also gives the employees regular opportunities to reflect upon their performance and strategize ways of improving, encouraging employees to improve week over week, month over month, and quarter over quarter — rather than simply year over year. All of these conversations should not only focus on technical job performance but also upon how well the employee is growing in their ability to embody Servant Leadership and the core values of your organization.

Then, when you do have formal, longer appraisal conversations, you can discuss the trajectory of the year in a more informed way. You know one another and can talk more freely and openly about areas of concern and causes for celebration. It's not a supervisor's job to be friends with their employees, but by being friendly you take fear out of the review process and replace it with the understanding that we're all on the same team here, working for the same goals, helping each other get better.

Of course, for this to work, Supervisors must be intentionally trained in how to provide meaningful performance feedback. They must learn to give (and receive) helpful feedback in a way that is honest, gentle, and fair. The damage that can come from poorly delivered performance feedback is just as significant as the damage that can come from no feedback at all. And poor performance feedback is often not a matter of bad information as it is a matter of good information delivered in a bad manner.

Untying compensation conversations from aspirational coaching allows supervisors to focus on how the employee can get better instead of manipulating the process to give the employee the raise they think is warranted. People can get anxious about money conversations, so remove that from the equation. This isn't about how much an employee makes; it's about how much better an employee can become.

Now, maybe you want to have a big, formal, data-centric and results-oriented performance coaching session once a year, with ongoing sessions provided by trained supervisors on an ongoing basis. That's fine. Nothing wrong with that. But this is a far cry from the currently typical Annual Performance Review. Aspirational performance coaching should be regular focused conversations aimed at helping people solve problems important to them and useful to your organization rather than a vague conversation about career goals and business objectives. And, above all, aspirational performance coaching must be delivered in a manner consistent with your Business Values and Servant Leadership philosophy.

Servant Leadership 360 Assessments Once Every Other Year

Psychologists and economists don't agree on much, but they all share the belief that the old adage is true:

You get what you measure.

Human beings tend to adjust their behavior based on whatever metrics they're held against. It happens organizationally and individually. If your standard of a successful school system is based on standardized test scores, guess what? You'll end up producing students who perform well on those tests. They may not perform well in other area, but they'll score well on the tests.

If a CEO believes his measurement of success is the stock price, that's what he'll focus on. He'll meet with people who have ideas about how to make that number go higher. He might buy something or sell something, hire someone or fire someone, in order to move that number. He'll do this even if he knows those actions are going to bite him later on.

And that gets us to our problem. How do you really measure leadership? Sadly, most organizations don't know how to do it, so they avoid doing it — which is dumb. The philosophy we've been advocating in this book posits that the true measure of a Servant Leader is found in the way he or she impacts those surrounding the leader. Consider again the six key questions for every Servant Leader:

Q 1. *Are all people with whom we interact being treated with dignity and respect as human beings?*

Q 2. *Are each of our team members growing as servant leaders and becoming more empowered, more knowledgeable, and more effective leaders?*

Q 3. *Are the weakest among us being helped by our service?*

Q 4. **Are we strengthening the trust of our employees and stakeholders that senior executives and the governing body actually walk the talk of servant leadership principles?**

Q 5. **Are we creating a culture that is authentically embracing the highest ideals of Servant Leadership at every level?**

Q 6. **Are we leading in a way that is constantly transforming the organization into who we aspire to become?**

Think how differently a leader's annual review would be if those were the core questions being asked. Of course, there must be a time when you examine the data. You want to make sure your leaders are being great financial stewards and consistently working towards a somewhat traditional understanding of success. But by now you know that this alone is insufficient.

So, maybe one way to help your organization stay on track and help your leaders fully embody your core values is to administer a Servant Leadership 360 every other year. You could offer people a chance to give (and receive) helpful feedback on how a leader is demonstrating specific behaviors and attitudes related to the 12 Characteristics of Servant Leaders.

Again, the evaluation here isn't tied to compensation or pay raises. Still, this is the kind of feedback a 4th Dimension Leader craves. Great leaders want to know how their behaviors are perceived by others.

For your review, here are those 12 Characteristics of Servant Leaders again:

LISTENING
When we think of leaders, we tend to think about great communicators or boldly decisive people who are willing and able to make the tough call when it counts. While those are vital skills for anyone in a position of authority, a Servant Leader lives out the phrase popularized by Stephen Covey, "Seek first to understand, then to be understood." Active listening is both a choice that must be made and a skill that must be continually developed in order to hear not only the words but the heart of the speaker as well.

EMPATHY
Such understanding, gained through actively listening to others, leads to empathy. Rather than demanding that others see things from my perspective, a Servant Leader is willing to stand in another's shoes. Certainly, I cannot ever do this perfectly; I do not have your perspective because I have not

had your experiences. Still, I want to communicate my desire to relate to the way another person experiences a particular situation and the context that has shaped that person's perspectives. To do this, I must always begin by giving the other person the benefit of the doubt, presuming that they are acting with good intentions.

HEALING

In many ways this principle — which Greenleaf believed to be the most powerful of all his principles — is a natural byproduct of combining the first two. A Servant Leader understands that how we treat people always has an emotional impact that is either positive or negative, either contributing positively to a person's overall health or damaging it. Because we understand this, we will strive to make the impact of our words and actions beneficial and uplifting — even when making difficult decisions regarding personnel. Your very presence as a Servant Leader can and should be healing.

AWARENESS

Awareness begins with self-awareness and extends to an awareness of the potential in others. It is more than just individual awareness, however. A Servant Leader is able to look at a situation and understand the politics and power plays at work, discerning the ethics and values at stake, and determining the best course of action. Good leaders know there is a gap between the ideal and the reality, and they feel a compelling need to act upon that awareness for the benefit of others.

PERSUASION

Servant Leaders do not primarily rely on coercion or positional authority. Instead, they understand that people are much more likely to support an idea if they have participated in the creation of it. This means all people are to be treated with respect and dignity as fellow human beings even if, and perhaps especially if, they disagree about the issue at hand. Rather than a coerced sense of compliance, persuasion creates a far more powerful sense of commitment.

CONCEPTUALIZATION
Servant Leaders are driven by a vision for the future that is better than the current reality. The dream big dreams, and they have the ability to articulate what the dream fulfilled will look like. Looking beyond the day-to-day operations, Servant Leaders keep those big, long range dreams in mind, planning day-to-day accordingly. Moreover, they are able to inspire others to visualize a better future for themselves as well. They inspire people to dream big dreams, and, in so doing, they create a shared vision that is worth sacrificing for in order to help it become a reality.

FORESIGHT
Tony Robbins has said, "Losers react; leaders anticipate." That may be a crass way of putting things, but one of the characteristics of a Servant Leader is the ability to understand lessons from the past, realities of the present, and the likely outcome of the current trajectory. This sense of insight and intuition gives one an ability to make good decisions in a VUCA world of volatility, uncertainty, complexity, and ambiguity. They may at times make decisions that followers do not fully understand, but trust nonetheless.

STEWARDSHIP
Because Servant Leaders are committed to serving the needs of others, they recognize that they have a responsibility to use

resources, achievements, and even influence in a way that preserves the good of now while providing a better future for others. While not ignoring current realities, the very essence of stewardship is long-term in context — it is impossible to be a good steward thinking only about the short-term.

COMMITMENT TO THE GROWTH OF PEOPLE

Servant leaders do not use people; they contribute to the growth of others. A Servant Leader has the underlying hope that every person he or she interacts with will be better off for having done so. This extends beyond their tangible contributions as employees, beyond their professional development to their personal development as well. The by-product of investing in the growth of people is an organization better prepared to thrive in a constantly changing world. An organization that is not a learning organization is doomed to mediocrity, and you cannot be a learning organization without investing in the constant growth of people.

BUILDING COMMUNITY

A Servant Leader ensures that, while goals are accomplished, they are never accomplished at the expense of relationships. On the contrary, Servant Leaders rely on the power of teams working in the context of authentic community. They recognize and honor the power of a sense of accountability, belonging, and care — the ABCs of authentic community. Indeed, healthy relationships are what allows an organization to stay at the leading edge of innovation.

CALLING

Servant Leaders have a natural desire to serve others and are willing to sacrifice self-interests for the sake of something bigger and more important than themselves. They long to make a difference in the lives of others. Added to this, as we've already mentioned, they can see things others cannot often see — namely, the gap between the ideal and the reality. In fact, Servant Leaders feel a burden to help close that gap. Doing so brings them a sense of joy and relief, even as it moves others into a better future. This double reward, both personal and global, draws them towards their destiny, towards the fulfillment of their deepest calling. It is that sense of calling that allows Servant Leaders to keep going when others might give into discouragement.

NURTURING THE SPIRIT

All of us have a deep human need to make a difference. Servant Leaders understand this and look for ways to help team members understand the difference they are making through honest praise and supportive recognition. Suggestions for improvement are offered in an honest and straightforward way, without harshness or personal attacks. Servant Leaders understand that most people want to be their best, although many do not understand how to achieve this and need direction, equipping, and encouragement to reach their full potential. Servant Leaders are not merely interested in helping an employee develop their professional skills. Rather, they realize that a person's spirit matters, too. When a person's spirit is nurtured and developed, work skills naturally improve, along with the work environment.

Servant Leadership Employee Engagement Assessments Once Every Other Year

On the years in which you don't conduct a Servant Leadership 360, the organization should conduct an assessment measuring employee engagement based upon the principles of Servant

Leadership. A recent study from Gallup has shown that only approximately 30% of the American workforce is fully engaged in their jobs. The complete impact of this startling reality goes far beyond economics and the stewardship of resources. Therefore, 4th Dimension Leadership requires us to create, measure, and refine ways to maintain employee engagement.

Typically, organizations will disseminate a survey where employees are asked to rate their own level of engagement. This approach offers insight into how engaged employees perceive themselves to be, and knowing what they think certainly has value. But, like most surveys, the reporting can vary day-to-day based on things like how an employee is feeling that day or whether or not Janice ate the last donut in the break room. There is the potential that respondents are only considering recent events. Also, it's likely that some will just tell you what they think you want to hear rather than what they believe is true.

A better approach will involve different data. You might consider taking a look at the amount of work that happens outside of normal working hours (evenings and weekends). You don't want to raise a generation of workaholics, but people who are highly engaged in something they believe is worthwhile will inevitably end up working a little extra. Also, try to get a feel for how often people participate in spontaneous meetings and initiatives versus recurring formal meetings and processes. If they're only involved in highly structured events, that can be an indicator of low engagement.

What you want is to figure out ways to measure actual engagement rather than self-perceived and self-reported engagement. You can also implement some cause-and-effect measures to boost engagement levels. For example, time spent in regular one-on-ones with their supervisor is directly linked to engagement. Engagement typically increases as an individual gets more time with his supervisor. Also, engagement can increase as people get more exposure to colleagues up the ladder, so time spent in the presence of skip-level leadership is important.

It shouldn't come as a big surprise that engagement typically decreases the more time people spend in very large group settings where it's difficult to feel like much more than an audience member. Try to limit meetings to fewer than 20 people. Also, make sure people have enough meaningful time to work between meetings and other events. Some of this is just common sense, and it may be more art than science. Ultimately, meetings aren't that productive if too many people are in the room or if there's not enough time to clear one's head between meetings.

Finally, remember that good, old-fashioned peer pressure is always at work. The engagement levels of colleagues is contagious. If you discover an employee who seems somewhat disengaged, rather than reprimanding them, assign them to a team filled with others who are more highly engaged.

Aspirational Coaching and Mentoring

Every future leader identifies role models, people from whom they learn how to lead. This can happen explicitly and intentionally, or it can happen implicitly and passively. And mark this down: every employee in your organization is learning about leadership from someone. The question is whether they are going to learn from a mentor who will help them become the kind of leader who will take your organization where you want it to go. If not, they will inevitably learn and perpetuate poor leadership skills from the "stealth incompetents" in your organization.

A formal process for mentoring employees and future leaders is foundational to developing a culture of exceptional leadership. The problem is that mentoring does not come naturally for most of us. Coaches and mentors must be carefully selected to ensure that they reflect the leadership skills and style you want emulated. They should receive training so they can do an effective job of mentoring. Being able to lead and being able to teach someone else how to lead are two different competencies. They can both be developed, but their development may only occur as a result of an intentional process.

Clear expectations for both parties must be established regarding engagement, interaction, and confidentiality. Ideally, a person should have an aspirational coach who is professionally trained in aspirational or executive coaching techniques and comes from another department, or even another organization. It always helps to have someone who is not a part of your immediate system, a person who has fresh eyes and a more objective perspective and still understands the basic principles of Servant Leadership.

PROMOTIONAL PROCESSES

Sustaining a Servant Leadership culture demands intentionality about who you promote and why. Far too often, people are promoted for technical competence when they have failed to develop leadership competence. These people end up frustrating their colleagues, demotivating employees, and institutionalizing mediocrity.

Promotional policies must take into account both attitude and aptitude. You cannot promote people who are technically competent but lack the qualities of a Servant Leader if you want to maintain a culture consistent with your core values. Technical competency should never be overlooked, but a 4th Dimension Leader must make a commitment not to promote people who are deficient when it comes to reflecting your Business Values no matter how technically competent they may be. Technical competency is the ante that gets you into the game, the "gimme" you start out with. It can never become the bar you're reaching for or the focus for promotions.

Ideally, your organization should not promote anyone until they have taken all the leadership development tracks appropriate for that position AND every level below it. For example, a front line employee who wants to become a supervisor shouldn't even be considered for promotion until they've demonstrated competency in all the Human Relations and Customer Service learning tracks at the Relational Leadership level, as well as all of the Supervisory learning tracks at the Operational Leadership level. A supervisor who wants to be promoted to a management position should have demonstrated competency in all of the learning tracks at the

Relational Leadership level, as well as the Supervisory and the Management learning at the Operational Leadership level.

Beyond technical and experiential qualifications, beyond having demonstrated competency in all of the leadership development learning tracks, promotional considerations should lean heavily upon performance capabilities as reflected in their performance coaching history and their effectiveness as a servant leader as reflected in their Servant Leadership 360s. Changing your promotional processes in this way will prevent the organization from becoming stagnant with supervisors and managers who fail to embody the Business Values and Servant Leadership culture in how they lead.

Walking the talk of Servant Leadership requires a long-term perspective and an understanding that decisions have consequences.

Promotional policies should overtly consider how effectively an employee makes decisions that advance the long-term health and well-being of the organization. The ideal candidate for promotion must have the vision to see beyond the current fiscal year.

A well designed leadership pipeline pays obvious dividends for the organization. You'll always have a strong talent pool to choose from, which means you'll reduce recruitment and turnover costs. You'll save as a result of the lowered learning curve that comes with hiring someone from outside of the organization and the risk of hiring outside candidates who are unknown entities. Plus, investing in the development of your people will raise their levels of engagement and morale because they'll know that they are valued and that you are investing in their future with your organization.

A SYSTEM OF SYSTEMS

The 4th Dimension Leadership Model sees the role of building systems as a critical part of excellent leadership. Without healthy systems in place, good intentions will never become effective practices. Worse, good intentions will soon sour, and you'll end up with a dysfunctional mess. The solution isn't to simply put new people (even if they are the right people) into your organization. A comprehensive system that supports and sustains the desired culture must be built and improved with relentless focus.

You will not be able to control your organizational destiny without building a system of systems that are all aligned with and reinforce your desired leadership culture and your Business Values.

A Final Thought

Jim Collins famously wrote, "Good is the enemy of great." This is certainly true when it comes to leadership development in your organization. The single biggest obstacle to creating an outstanding leadership development program is the existence of an acceptably adequate program. Honestly, no one wants to be called "adequate".

- *How's that new car?* Adequate.
- *How was your dinner?* Adequate.
- *How was your honeymoon?* Adequate.

Can you imagine? Adequate. Good enough. Meh. Adequate is boring. No one wants adequate. No one sets out to create an adequate program. And yet, we settle for adequate in the one factor that will has the greatest influence on the long-term success and vitality of our organization: leadership development.

In some strange way adequate creates a kind of inertia that resists change — no matter how badly we know change is needed. We know the status quo cannot be maintained long-term. We know one day it will catch up to us. And yet we persist in propping up adequate systems hoping…for what? That something magical will happen?

The first step to creating a great leadership development program is the willingness to confront the reality that adequate is no longer acceptable.

Most great change only comes after you begin to feel what Bill Hybels calls "a holy discontent". When you decide that good enough is no longer good enough and begin to demand excellence - then you can begin to create something excellent.

Developing leaders is the single most important responsibility an executive bears.

Excellence in this area is essential for the long-term vitality and viability of your organization. And excellence doesn't just happen. Excellence requires commitment. Excellence requires a long-range perspective. You have to be clear on what excellence will look like when it shows up. And you must have a coherent and carefully executed game plan for turning your vision into a reality.

In today's VUCA world, a radical style of authentic leadership which balances the constructive tension between returning to the roots of healthy, high-trust relationships between leaders and followers and stretching the team to be innovative and dynamic, embracing change out on the leading edge — this is what is demanded.

Servant Leadership provides the philosophical foundation for this radical balancing act, while the 4th Dimension Leadership Model provides a practical framework for reforming organizational systems in a way that can make cultural transformation a sustainable reality.

Combined, they will help you stop settling for adequate.

CPSIA information can be obtained
at www.ICGtesting.com
Printed in the USA
LVHW04s1803050718
582794LV00001B/18/P